© Copyright 2019, Etienne de la Boetie²

A copyright, as pointed out by Larken Rose, is usually an implied threat: ("Don't Copy This or Else!"). Like Larken, I hope that anyone who likes this book will buy additional copies from me to help fund our experiment in large-scale cult deprogramming. If someone does copy it without permission then that alone would not make me feel justified in using force against that person, on my own or using "government" as my proxy. If someone was uncool enough to sell bootleg copies then I have no doubt that karma, always operating at maximum power in the universe, would kick their ass far more effectively than any government lackey. Like Larken, I have copyrighted the book primarily so no one else can copyright it and use the violence of the state to prevent me from distributing it. – Etienne de la Boetie²

Fair Use Act Disclaimer

FAIR USE
Copyright Disclaimer under section 107 of the Copyright Act 1976, allowance is made for "fair use" for purposes such as criticism, comment, news reporting, teaching, scholarship, education and research. Fair use is a use permitted by copyright statute that might otherwise be infringing.

FAIR USE DEFINITION:
Fair use is a doctrine in the United States copyright law that allows limited use of copyrighted material without requiring permission from the rights holders, such as for commentary, criticism, news reporting, research, teaching or scholarship. It provides for the legal, non-licensed citation or incorporation of copyrighted material in another author's work.

Pro-Tip:
This book is best read and gifted as a hard copy. If you really want someone to spend time with a written work then paper is the most inviting, impossible to delete, easier on the eyes, and convenient. For a dual-sided printer select: Landscape, Print on Both Sides of the Paper, and: Flip on the Short Side. A double sided printer will require 66 pages and a single sided print will require 132 pages of paper. Please let this notice memorialize our permission to have this book reprinted at copy shops and office supply stores where you can have it spiral bound or perfect bound.

ISBN
978-1-64606-296-6 – Softcover
978-1-64606-295-9 – Ebook

Executive Summary of the Executive Summary

"Government" wasn't designed to protect life, liberty and property. It is a system, a technique used by inter-generational organized crime to rob and control society. The only reason anyone believes it is legitimate, desirable, or necessary is because they have been indoctrinated into the belief system from birth through mandatory government schools, control of private school curriculum through accreditation, scouting, military/police "training" and a propaganda system of six monopoly media companies running hundreds of subsidiaries to give the illusion of choice and diversity of opinion. Google/YouTube/Facebook/Twitter/Amazon/Wikipedia/Reddit/Meet-Up/Disqus/Netflix/Instagram/Snopes further control perception on the DARPA Internet by creating a "propaganda matrix" that the system is legitimate while distracting the population and hiding/denigrating the news outlets, websites, documentaries, and videos that are exposing the criminality of the system.

The Good News

You aren't an "American" or a "Russian" or an "Israeli" just because you were born in one geographical area or another. You are a free and sentient human being who doesn't owe your income or allegiance to any organized crime system using classical, textbook unethically manipulative cult-indoctrination techniques on an unsuspecting public. The world is a self-organizing system that produces spontaneous order and all the legitimate, non-redistributive functions the "government" performs such as armed protective services, dispute resolution, roads, schools, and air traffic control could be better provided by the free market and real charity or likely shouldn't be done at all. Voluntaryism I.E. *real* freedom, has been the biggest secret that has been kept from society and misrepresented by the monopoly propaganda system because it is the only political system that is fair for all. No one gets the "ring of power"... No one gets to use violence or extortion on anyone else... Not even "government". After you free your own mind from what was force fed you in your youth then free just 5 other people and then we are all free. Hopefully this book and our dropbox/flash drives/data DVD Liberators can help.

– *Etienne de la Boetie[2]*

Contents

Preparing the Reader	5
Introduction	6
The 20+ Techniques That Create Mental/Tax Slavery	9
#1 - Flag: Artificial Indoctrinated Holy Symbol	9
#2 - Constitutions and Bills of Rights	10
#3 - Mandatory government schools employing the Prussian model of education	11
#4 - Youth Programs to teach "citizenship", blind obedience and state/flag worship	13
#5 - Youth programs to militarize children	15
#6 - Pledges and oaths are forced on Kids	17
#7 - Military and police are artificially glorified and celebrated	18
#8 - Political Rallies and Politician Worship	19
#9 - Use of Propaganda	20
#10 - Use of manufactured news, overt or surreptitious control of publishers, editors, and reporters creates an "artificial reality."	21
#11 - Use of Manufactured Terrorism	22
#12 - Use of False Flag events, manufactured intelligence and lies to start wars	23
#13 - Secret government/real power structure's use of political assassinations of rivals, whistle blowers and dissidents	24
#14 - Political "Temples" dedicated to the State and its deities	25
#15 - Monopoly Government Fiat Money Steals Value Secretly from the Population	26
#16 - Spying on Citizens	27
#17 - Torture as Policy	28
#18 - Secret Prisons, For-profit prisons (for victimless crimes), Concentration Camps, and "Black Sites"	29
#19 - Use of conscription to forcefully enslave people to fight wars and further indoctrinate them into the government's ideology and discipline	30
#20 - Manufactured Enemies to unite the population under the government	
#21 - Use of paid political violence at the rallies of their political opposition	31

One-Pagers	32
Propaganda Using Religious Symbolism	32
The Religion of Statism	34
The Shady History of the *Con*-stitution	36
The Shady History of the Pledge of Allegiance	38
Public (Government) School Indoctrination	40
The Private Federal Reserve and Theft of Fractional Reserve Banking	42
The Propaganda Matrix	44
Control of the media and, by extension, human perception	46
Organized Crime's Front Groups & Secret Societies	48
Consumer Monopoly Consolidation	50
Understanding Genetically Modified Organisms (GMOs) and Monopoly Seed Consolidation	52
Anarchy and Voluntaryism – The Biggest Secret in American Politics	54
False Flag Terrorism for War and Domestic Police State	56
The Basics for Police, Judges, and Government Employees	58
Please Help Free These Political Prisoners	60
Whistleblowers, Confessions, and Quotes	61
Meme War	63
The Basics	63
The Ridiculousness, Illogic, and Immorality of "Government" and "Democracy"	66

Contents

Liberty Hacks & Solutions	82
Spiritual Health & Wellness	86
Culture War	90
Take Back and (Ultimately) Privatize the Government School System	92
Buy Local	95
Is Amazon really A Mason? The case for organized crime	95
Get Together and Get Concentrated	97
Liberty Events Calendar	99
Preparedness and Crypto-Currencies	100
Freedom Apps, Blockchain, and Crypto Projects for Digital Liberty	103
FIVE - Our movement & advice for a voluntary society	111
Thoughts on strategy	112
The Art of Liberty Foundation	113
The Pre-State Project	114
The Liberator – Our Flash Drive of Liberty Resources	115
The Symbolism Behind the Liberator	116
Large Scale Cult Deprogramming & Uncensorable Hand-to-Hand Distribution	117
What, Why, and How to Help	
Statism is a Cult! Complete Breakdown with Examples	118
The Art of Liberty Foundation Strategy	119
Get the Understanding Our Slavery Poster for your High School or College Classroom	121
International Editions - On the Horizon	122
Packages	123
Sponsorship/Donation/Order Form	125
How to Help with CryptoCurrency	126
Dedication & Acknowledgements	127
Connect with Us on E-mail and Social Media	128
The History of the Etienne de la Boetie2 Nom de Plume	129

Preparing the Reader

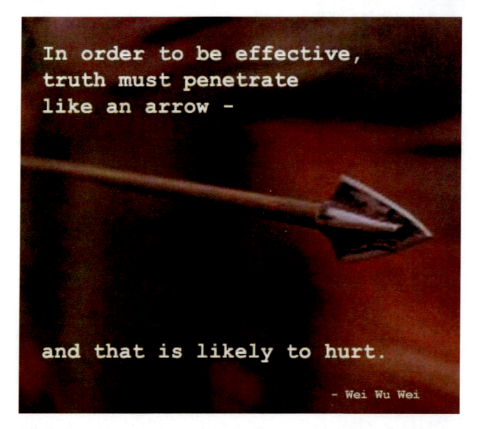

For many, especially those who work for the "government", police or serve/served in the military, what you are going to learn in this book is going to be painful. If you read with an open mind and you are able to take a step back and analyze what you were told as a child about the *legitimacy, desirability, necessity* and *morality* of "Government" you are going to discover that you were tricked... By mandatory schools, scouting and a multi-trillion dollar control-of-perception program of monopoly media and algorithmic censorship on the DARPA Internet... *Just like this author was for decades...* into supporting a system based on *lies, propaganda, indoctrination, extortion and violence.* The reward comes in knowing the truth because the truth shall, quite literally, *set you free.* - To admit that one is wrong is to declare that you are wiser now than you were before.

"There are three classes of people: those who see, those who see when they are shown, those who do not see" **- Leonardo Da Vinci**

Introduction

Techniques for controlling populations have been developed and honed by monarchies, despots, tyrants, and "democratic governments" for centuries. The U.S. government today does not remotely resemble or respect the ideals of the original republic, which the government school system still celebrates and pretends exists. It now parallels the <u>same system</u> that was used to control the tax slaves/ actual slaves in Nazi Germany, the Soviet Union and East Germany. In addition to sharing mechanisms of control and indoctrination, **these governments are all illegitimate because it is impossible to delegate rights you don't have personally to "representatives."** For example, If you don't have the moral right to coerce money from your neighbor and redistribute it to others, then you can't delegate that "right" to a "representative" — even if the majority agrees. Voting can't change morality, and just because the mob wants to lynch black folks or rob Peter to pay Paul, it doesn't mean those actions are legitimate by 'virtue' of the majority outnumbering its victims.

Unfortunately, using violence to rob and control society is organized crime, and the control system known as "government" has always been used to fleece the population. Those in power have tended to use the same techniques through history. They control educational institutions and the media to perpetuate propaganda and indoctrinate the pseudo-religion of Statism into children. <u>Statism</u> is the propagandized belief in the ***necessity***, ***desirability***, and ***legitimacy*** of "government". It is a mind control technique and pseudo-religion because there is no such thing as "government."

You can't go to Washington D.C./ "Mecca" and touch "government!" You can touch buildings and people, but "government" is just an ***idea***. It is a "supernatural entity" that promises to make the world a better place: to feed the poor, to protect the weak, and to provide for your retirement. It can even raise wages and lower prices at the same time! Is there nothing the State can't do?

Pursuant to government power, free children are brought up in mandatory schools believing that because they were born on this side or that side of an imaginary line (a border), they are "American" or "Canadian," for example, and — by virtue of where they were born — now owe half their income in overt/covert taxes and inflation to organized crime using well-recognized and unethically manipulative "cult indoctrination" techniques and propaganda on them. Some cult members are so mind-controlled they even shave their heads, wear costumes, and murder whomever the cult leaders tell them to or lock peaceful people in for-profit prisons for victimless crimes.

The idea that Americans are "free" when they are forced to pay as much as half their income in overt taxes, covert taxes, and inflation while putting up with the government's myriad rules, regulations, monopolies and licensing schemes borders on ludicrous.

"Americans" are victims of a multi-trillion dollar con-game through which they have been indoctrinated and secretly propagandized into an artificial belief system that teaches them to be "tax-payers" and some to be "order-followers" to kill and enforce on their fellow tax slaves. It is a system based on lies, brainwashing, propaganda, and the immoral, poisonous idea that some people can be "delegated" the "authority" to rule others. The acceptance of the legitimacy of "authority" is the acceptance that you are a slave and must obey a master. The difference between a free man and a slave is that slaves can't say: **No.**

***Real* Freedom! - The alternative that is often paid lip service but rarely offered in government schools:** It amounts to no masters, no slaves! One of the biggest secrets kept from public (government) school children is that the world is a self-organizing system that produces spontaneous order and that all the "services" provided by government — from protection to roads to charity — can be better provided by voluntary interaction, the free market, and real charity. Freedom doesn't guarantee utopia, but it is the most moral alternative that unleashes the creativity and capital creation mechanisms of the market. Voluntaryism/anarchism are social movements that reject the artificially indoctrinated belief system of Statism in favor of true freedom and voluntary interactions between free people. It is the most moral and principled of all the political systems in that it recognizes **natural law vs. frequently immoral and illogical Government law (I.E. "politician scribbles")** and honors the **Non-Aggression Principle (NAP)**, which posits that no individual or group of individuals has the right to initiate violence and coercion against other human beings who are not aggressing against them — in other words, live and let live, unless someone is threatening your life or property. All other political philosophies (socialism, communism, monarchy, democracy, constitutional republicanism, etc.) allow a ruling class to engage in violence and coercion against the majority. Though these systems may even allow elections where the winning party is allowed to rob everyone in society to enact its stated political goals, elections amount to ritualistic theater (especially when they only represent a minority of the eligible voters and the winner was outnumbered by citizens who didn't vote at all). In addition to the travesty that occurs when majority rule tramples the rights of the minority, elections are also easily rigged and controlled by moneyed interests to offer the illusion of control to the tax slaves who are ignorant/willfully ignorant of the 'big con'.

20+ techniques used by inter-generational organized crime to create the cult-ure of slavery/tax slavery and how it manifested in each time and place.

Nazi Germany	US Government Current	Soviet Union/Russia	East Germany
1933-1945	1776-Present	1922-1991	1949-1990

Flag: Artificial Indoctrinated Holy Symbol - Flags evolved from war banners that war parties carried in battle. Symbolically, they are the same as the "colors" of crips, bloods, and other gangs. Today flags are used by organized crime governments to indoctrinate populations into the local flavor of Statism as a pseudo-religious artificial holy symbol. In the U.S., children are forced to pledge their allegiance with their hands over their hearts starting in kindergarten in mandatory schools. Cub Scouts, Boy Scouts, military academies, and police/military training further reinforce this artificial reverence with artificial solemn rituals: how the holy flag should be folded, carried, saluted, buried, and ultimately revered. Organized crime's media system reinforces this religiosity by product-placing the flag into hundreds of movies and television shows that becomes painfully obvious in this [short video showing 469 "product placements" in just 12 Michael Bay movies](). Hollywood propagandists frequently use a technique called "Anchoring" where they create a moment of high positive emotion [(Matt Damon escaping Mars in the Martian) and then "Anchor" that exhilaration to the flag by immediately cutting to people on earth waving American flags]() or waiting for a player to score a touchdown and then cutting to the flag or to military/police personnel celebrating in the audience. The NBA has added the flag to their backboards to "anchor" the exhilaration of a goal and the NFL to helmets where players are forbidden to remove them.

Type of Government

| Republic | Republic | Republic | Republic |

Nazi Germany	US Government Current	Soviet Union/Russia	East Germany

Constitutions and Bills of Rights - Most governments pretend there is a "social contract" between the people and the government (organized crime) under which the people are guaranteed certain rights. But the organized crime governments always break these agreements, and there is really no agreement at all since these one-sided contracts are simply forced on the populations. Ultimately, even the most oppressive governments pretend to have "constitutions" and declarations of "rights." Abolitionist and legal theorist Lysander Spooner completely decimated the moral and legal legitimacy of the US Constitution in 1867 with [No Treason: The Constitution of No Authority](#) whose arguments are just as relevant today.

Yes	Yes	Yes	Yes
		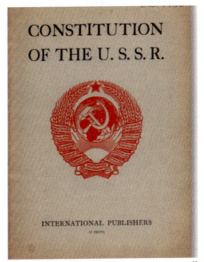	
The **Constitution of the German Reich** usually known as the **Weimar Constitution** (Weimarer Verfassung) was the constitution that governed Germany from 1919 to 1945. It had all kinds of guaranteed rights (assembly, freedom of religion, press, etc.) all ignored.	The idea that you owe up to ½ of your income to the government in overt taxes, covert taxes, and inflation, all because hundreds of years ago a couple dozen slave-owners on a continent of three million people wrote down on a piece of paper that they alone get to make up rules for everyone and steal the wealth of others is not credible. [US Government constantly ignores its own Bill of Rights.](#)	The "Stalin Constitution" adopted December 5th, 1936. Article 125 of the constitution guaranteed freedom of speech, of the press, and of assembly. All ignored.	Draft of the East German constitution, March 1949. Article 8 guaranteed personal liberty, inviolability of one's dwelling, personal effects, and papers. All ignored.

Nazi Germany	US Government Current	Soviet Union/Russia	East Germany

Mandatory government schools employing the Prussian model of education - Such schools were developed specifically and openly to indoctrinate obedience and fealty to king, country, and "government." *"The new education must consist essentially in this, that it completely destroys freedom of will in the soil which it undertakes to cultivate, and produces on the contrary strict necessity in the decisions of the will the opposite being impossible."* – Johanne Fichte, Architect of the Prussian System, *Addresses to the German Nation 1807* The government's mandatory school system appears to have three hidden curriculums:

Statism – Teaching students that government is legitimate, moral, necessary and desirable before they are old enough to evaluate the logic and morality of the claim while using unethically manipulative cult-indoctrination techniques: The "common prayer" of the Pledge of Allegiance and national anthem, Prussian model of education, government-affiliated scouting programs, and JROTC, focus on Presidents (Popes), class trips to Washington DC (Mecca) where the children are taken into the "cathedral" of the Capital and the "temples" to see the "deities" and holy documents.

Obedience – Subtle techniques that forever condition children into obedience to "authority" and submission to "government": Drill bells, walking in lines, active shooter drills requiring permission to use restroom, assigned seating, warrantless searches, public shaming, collective punishment, Red, Yellow, Green "troublemaker boards" and socialization of the monopoly police through school "resource officers" and the D.A.R.E. program.

Debilitation – Mandatory mercury and aluminum-laced vaccines, ADD/ADHD "medications", fluoridated water in the water fountain, and glyphosate-soaked and GMO garbage food in the cafeteria.

| Yes | Yes | Yes | Yes |
|---|---|---|---|//
|  |  |  |  |

Nazi Germany	US Government Current	Soviet Union/Russia	East Germany
Mandatory government schools employing the Prussian model of education			
"The whole function of education is to create Nazis" - **Bernhard Rust - Minister of Education in Nazi Germany**, "He alone who owns the youth gains the future" - **Adolph Hitler**	The U.S. government's mandatory schools adopted/used the socialist "Bellamy/Nazi Salute" until 1943, at which point the crimes of the National Socialist "Nazi" Party in Germany became apparent. "Diet, injections, and injunctions {Schooling – Ed} will combine, from a very early age, to produce the sort of character and the sort of beliefs that the authorities consider desirable, and any serious criticism of the powers that be will become psychologically impossible."- **Bertrand Russell**, Fabian Socialist and Eugenicist writing in *The Impact of Science on Society*, 1953	"Education is a weapon, whose effect depends on who holds it in his hands and at whom it is aimed." – **Joseph Stalin** "The education of all children, from the moment that they can get along without a mother's care, shall be in state institutions." - **Karl Marx**	When children entered their classrooms at the beginning of each day, almost every teacher would ask the pupils 'Seid bereit?' (Are you willing?), which was responded by 'Immer bereit' (Always prepared). Every class had a class council with a sitting president and vice president who indoctrinated and habituated their fellow students into statism.

| Nazi Germany | US Government Current | Soviet Union/Russia | East Germany |

<u>Youth Programs to teach "citizenship", blind obedience and state/flag worship</u> - To this day, the Prussian education model is used on children as the first level of indoctrination. Government-affiliated scouting programs are the 2nd level, at which point children receive awards (Cub Scout Adventure Loops, Boy Scout Merit Badges, etc.) for learning and demonstrating their conditioning: Duties as a "citizen," reverence for/worship of the flag, pride of uniform, obedience to hierarchical command over conscience and basic morality, and other techniques that ultimately produce "order followers" willing to kill upon orders from the State.

In the US the Boy Scouts of America has been funded in recent years by banks, cartel companies, and defense contractors dependent on fractional reserve banking, government monopolies, mandatory vaccines and government contracts including **Banks**: JP Morgan, Bank of America, Wells Fargo, US Bank **Cartel Companies**: Verizon (warrantless wiretapping) Monsanto (chemical weapons, toxins in food supply) **Vaccine Makers**: Abbot, Merck, Pfizer, Eli Lilly (mercury-laced vaccine preservative Thimerosal) **Defense Contractors**: GE (also owns NBC), Dow Chemical, Lockheed Martin.

Recent National Presidents have included: **Randall Stephenson** (Former CEO of defense/intelligence agency contractor and warrantless wiretapper AT&T, CFR Member) **Robert Gates** (Former CIA, Sec of Defense, CFR Member, Reported Bilderberg attendee in 2011 in violation of the Logan Act, and reported Bohemian Club speaker) and **Norman Augustine** (CEO of defense contractor Lockheed Martin, co-founder of CIA investment fund In-Q-Tel, and CFR member, Bohemian Club Member). Honorary Vice Presidents include: **George W. Bush**, **Bill Clinton** and **Barack Obama**.

| Hitler Youth | Boy Scouts of America | Russian Young Pioneers | East German Young Pioneers |

Nazi Germany	US Government Current	Soviet Union/Russia	East Germany
<td colspan="4">**Youth Programs to teach "citizenship," blind obedience to hierarchical authority over conscience and basic morality and State/flag worship**</td>			
Hitler Youth	**Boy Scouts of America**	**Russian Young Pioneers**	**East German Young Pioneers**
"These boys and girls enter our organizations [at] ten years of age, and often for the first time get a little fresh air; after four years of the Young Folk they go on to the Hitler Youth, where we have them for another four years … And even if they are still not complete National Socialists, they go to Labor Service and are smoothed out there for another six, seven months … And whatever class consciousness or social status might still be left … the Wehrmacht [German armed forces] will take care of that." —Adolf Hitler (1938)	The Scouting program is steeped in statism. Baden-Powell himself was an authoritarian whose vision of his fledgling program was to train boys in militaristic fashion with the virtues that militaries focus on and foster. "A Scout is loyal to the King" and his subordinates, Baden-Powell wrote. "He must stick to them through thick and thin against anyone who is their enemy, or who even talks badly of them." Unsurprisingly, unquestioning and submissive obedience is another "Scout law" Baden-Powell created. "A Scout obeys orders… without question. Even if he gets an order he does not like, he must do as soldiers and sailors do, he must carry it out all the same *because it is his duty*…" (emphasis in the original).	Vladimir Lenin All-Union Pioneer Organization

"To be accepted as a Pioneer each child had to promise: …In the presence of my comrades I solemnly promise: to love and cherish my Motherland passionately, to live as the great Lenin bade us, as the Communist Party teaches us, and as required by the laws of the Young Pioneers of the Soviet Union." | Used to indoctrinate children as members of a new socialist society, both the Young Pioneers and Free German Youth were imposed by authorities to attack religious beliefs and, ultimately, divide children from their family and many of their values. Kids were forced to join if they wanted to have any chance of being accepted into institutions of higher learning. |

Nazi Germany	US Government Current	Soviet Union/Russia	East Germany

Youth programs to militarize children – These are a subset of the main program (Explorers in the US Boy Scouts) in which some children are militarized and indoctrinated to accept hierarchical command and control, more obedience to authority, military training, flag worship, pride of uniform, and obedience to federal "authorities," among other submissive qualities. Every branch of the military has its own Military Explorer Program and a reported 500,000 kids participate in Explorers, JROTC, Young Marines, and DoD starbase. Law Enforcement Explorers condition kids starting in 6th grade into accepting government monopoly policing with ride-alongs, meetings, and uniforms. In 2001 it was reported that there were almost 2000 posts and 32,000 14-21 year olds participating. From my review of the curriculum there is no discussion on the morality of incarcerating overwhelmingly peaceful people for victimless crimes, the for-profit prison system, or living off money stolen at the point of a gun. Federal and military involvement includes academy programs run by the FBI, DEA, Secret Service, Border Patrol, and Military Police. A 2011 L.A. Weekly investigation revealed that the Law Enforcement Explorer program alone had over 100 incidents of participating police officers engaging in sex with participants with the overwhelming majority being underage.

| Hitler Youth | Boy Scouts of America / Young Marines | The Komsomol | Free German Youth Movement |
|---|---|---|---|//
|  |  |  |  |

Nazi Germany	US Government Current	Soviet Union/Russia	East Germany
Youth programs to Militarize children			
Hitler Youth	**Boy Scouts of America**	**The Komsomol**	**Free German Youth Movement**
Hitler created the Hitler Youth because, as he believed, "The weak must be chiselled away. I want young men and women who can suffer pain. Part of the boys training was to part of their "military athletics" (Wehrsport) included marching, bayonet drills, grenade throwing, trench digging, map reading, gas defense, use of dugouts, how to get under barbed wire, and pistol shooting.	The Boy Scouts of America Explorer program is now working with the Department of Homeland Security, U.S. Military, and individual police forces to train hundreds of thousands of kids and instill in them the glory of being a government enforcer and serving in the Empire's armies of occupation. Over 500,000 US kids in Junior ROTC with the military running dozens of public high schools including 8 in Chicago alone. Young Marines and Dod Starbase programs target elementary and middle school kids under the guise of STEM education.	The Komsomol included indoctrination through social work and sport, communal living, "red christenings," and books and cinema. In addition to taking part in various military physical education drills, children were also required to have the ability to assemble and disassemble an AK-47 in under 30 seconds.	East German Young Pioneers graduated into the Free German Youth movement (Freie Deutsche Jugend / FDJ), which included military training. Meetings were normally scheduled so they overlapped with Catholic ceremonies and gatherings. This was the consequence of an effort to veer young minds away from religious morals and customs that may have worked against communist war tactics.

Nazi Germany	US Government Current	Soviet Union/Russia	East Germany

Pledges and oaths are forced on Kids: Thousands and thousands or repetitions are required in mandatory government schools and government-sponsored youth programs from a young age. While U.S. children can sit down for the pledge, peer pressure and the "authority" of the government school teachers and scout "masters" ensures conformity.

Nazi Germany	US Government Current	Soviet Union/Russia	East Germany
Yes	Yes	Yes	Yes
Hitler Youth Pledge of Allegiance: "We carry the flag forward into the battle of the youth. It stands and is raised and blazes to the heavens like fire in the sky. We are sworn to be true to the flag for all eternity. Whosoever shall desecrate the flag will be cursed for all eternity. The flag is our belief in God, People, and Country. Whoever seeks to destroy it must first take our lives and prosperity. We care for the flag as a mother cares for her child. The flag is our future, our honor, and the source of our courage."	**US Pledge of Allegiance** "I pledge allegiance to the Flag of the United States of America, and to the Republic for which it stands, one Nation under God, indivisible, with liberty and justice for all."	I (surname, given name), having now joined the ranks of the Vladimir Illich Lenin All-Union Pioneer Organization, in the presence of my comrades solemnly promise: to passionately love my fatherland and to cherish it as I can, to live, study, and fight as the Great Lenin has instructed, as the Communist Party teaches me, and as to always carry out the laws of the Pioneers of the Soviet Union.	"Ernst Thälmann is my model. I promise to learn to work and to fight as Ernst Thälmann teaches. I will follow the rules of the Thälmann Pioneers. True to our greeting, I am always ready to support peace and socialism."

Nazi Germany	US Government Current	Soviet Union/Russia	East Germany

Military and police are artificially glorified and celebrated - In the U.S., the government, the propaganda system, and affiliated cartel companies promote the sanctity of the military with preferred parking, discounts, priority boarding at the airport, ceremonies at stadium events, etc. These benefits and rituals promote militarism so the slaves are propagandized to worship the enforcers. Often, those perpetuating these practices and delusions believe in them wholeheartedly themselves. In the soldiers' defense, many join the military with the best of intentions and are awake to the criminality of how they are being used.

Yes	Yes	Yes	Yes

This image shows the military being celebrated before a soccer game in Nazi Germany.	The US Government has been caught paying professional sports teams over $53 million to include pro-military / pro-gov't messages during games/"circuses." The media propaganda system (news, film, and television) portrays the military as heroic for invading and occupying foreign lands in wars based on lies and manufactured intelligence.	Every 9th of May is victory day in Russia and celebrates Russian military victories. It normally includes a grand spectacle showcasing the newest weapons in the nation's arsenal.	It's almost like they all use the same techniques, eh?

Nazi Germany	US Government Current	Soviet Union/Russia	East Germany

Political Rallies and Politician Worship use spectacle, Neurolingustic Programming speech techniques, the use of the artificially, indoctrinated holy symbol of the flag, slogans/propaganda, and often participants who are paid/bussed in to give the illusion of grass-roots support/popularity for tell-a-vision cameras while conditioning individuals into groupthink, and the "common prayer" of Statism using similar techniques as religious revivals.

Yes	Yes	Yes	Yes

The participants frequently engage in worship of the artificially created/promoted political leader "savior" not understanding that the organized crime system is leveraging knowledge of human psychology to exploit most, but not all, humans' biological desire for a leader/"father figure" and inclusion in the artificially created "tribe" I.E. country.

Nazi Germany	US Government Current	Soviet Union/Russia	East Germany

Use of Propaganda – The government conspires with the entertainment industry to sell the population on nationalism and the "legitimacy" of the tax slavery system. As with militarism, many of those perpetuating these ideas believe them, too. Much is subtle… countless movies and tell-a-vision shows support the "legitimacy" of government and the status quo, modeling behavior on how the public is "supposed" to behave in certain situations like court or police encounters. Good-looking, ripped, government employees (FBI/CIA/DEA/ATF/POTUS/FWS/Military/Police) always save the day. "Product placement" of the US flag and militarism abounds in Hollywood's content and is often directly sponsored and influenced by government agencies.

The Nazi party established a film division as early as 1930. Nazi propaganda minister Joseph Goebbels appointed himself "Patron of the German film" and promoted escapism, exercised censorship over news, and funded films that showed the Nazi party in a positive light. Distributed "People's Receivers" radios limited in range to only receive Nazi (not foreign) broadcasts which were outlawed.	CIA and Dept of Defense have direct involvement in 800+ major movies and 1000+ television shows: Argo, Zero Dark Thirty, and others shape a false paradigm. NPR & "Public Television" is also used to distract and deceive. Product placement of the American flag "anchored" to moments of high positive emotion is found in movies like The Martian or every Michael Bay movie.	The main Soviet censorship body, Glavlit, was employed not only to eliminate any undesirable printed materials, but also to ensure that the correct ideological spin was put on every published item. In the Stalin era, deviation from the dictates of official propaganda was punished by execution and labor camps. Only two permitted news organizations: Pravda ("Truth") and Izvestia ("The News").	One Stasi propaganda film targeting kids, The Sun Always Lives, showed children as young as five in miniature tanks. At the end of the film, a live shell from one of the mini-tanks hits a wall. At this point the voice-over for the film says: "Show your soldierly face for the Socialist Fatherland as these brave warriors do!"

Nazi Germany	US Government Current	Soviet Union/Russia	East Germany

<u>Use of manufactured news, overt or surreptitious control of publishers, editors, and reporters creates an "artificial reality."</u> In the U.S., six monopoly "news" and entertainment companies running hundreds of subsidiaries give the illusion of choice, while Bilderberg attendees, members of the Council on Foreign Relations, and Trilateral Commission members hold key editorial positions at major wire services, networks, and newspapers. About two dozen new media companies funded to consolidate their competition to control search, social media, comments, "fact-checking", and news on the DARPA Internet.

Yes	Yes	Yes	Yes

Newspapers
- **Censoring** newspapers ensures that only the news you want people to read is available to the public
- October 1933 new law made editors responsible for infringements of government directives
- Clause 14 obliged editors to exclude anything 'calculated to weaken the strength of the Reich'
- **Treason** to spread false news or rumours
- Many **publications banned.**
    ....1933 there were 4,700 daily newspapers, 3% controlled by NSDP (Nazi party)
    ....1944 there were only 997 daily newspapers, 82% of which were controlled by NSDP.

Radio
1) The **Peoples Receiver** – limited range in order to only hear Nazi broadcasts (could not pick up foreign broadcasts)
-All news broadcasts came through the Nazi Office of Propaganda
-Between 1932-9 the number of families with radios rose from 25% to 70%
-Goebbels described radio as "*the spiritual weapon of the totalitarian state*"

SlideShare on Nazi Propaganda Techniques
http://www.slideshare.net/chrishume/nazi-propaganda-1003819

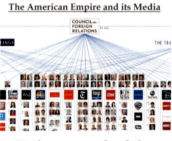
CIA's control of the press, Operation Mockingbird/"Mighty Wurlitzer", was exposed in the Church Committee hearings (1976) where it came out that the CIA was paying hundreds of reporters/editors for "product placement" of agency propaganda.
2017 American Empire and Its Media
2011 F.R.E.E chart shows CFR, TC and Bilderberg control of the press.

Stalin famously had murdered Soviet leaders air-brushed out of pictures

Just one channel: The Government's channel…

Nazi Germany	US Government Current	Soviet Union/Russia	East Germany

Use of Manufactured Terrorism - This is a technique used throughout history to unite populations behind the government against manufactured external enemies. FBI provided the explosives to its informant Emad Salem in 1993 WTC bombing and FBI/ATF #1 suspects in OKC bombing. Al-Qaeda and ISIS/ISIL are proxy armies funded and controlled by intelligence agencies at the top, and many of the "beheading videos" and other filmed atrocities are cartoonish and obviously fake. They are designed to play on American fears; for example, it was recently revealed that the Pentagon paid British P.R. firm Bell Pottenger $540M to create fake terrorist propaganda films.

Yes	Yes	Yes	No Known Cases
It is widely believed that the Nazi Party burned down their own parliament building (The Reichstag fire) and blamed the incident on their political competitors, the communists, to seize power.	**Domestic:** OKC bombing, 9-11, **Hundreds** of FBI agent-provocateured domestic terror plots to create the illusion of "terrorism" to justify "gov't" existence. **Foreign:** Al-Qaeda/ISIS, are CIA proxy armies. Operation Gladio created false flag terror in Europe. The Phoenix Program in Vietnam.	Russian Apartment Bombings In 1999, a series of apartment bombings were blamed on Chechen separatists, but the explosives and a car used by the perpetrators were traced back to the FSB — the Russian Federal Security Service. Post-Soviet Era	

Nazi Germany	US Government Current	Soviet Union/Russia	East Germany

Use of False Flag events, manufactured intelligence and lies to start wars - A false flag is when a country, usually through its intelligence services, manufactures an apparent/actual attack from another country or a terrorist event to unite the public behind the government, restrict civil liberties, and benefit politically-connected firms, military industrial complex companies and banking interests.

Yes	**Yes**	**Yes**	**No**
The Gleiwitz Incident was designed to create the illusion that Poland was aggressing against Germany. It started when German operatives led by Alfred Naujocks seized the radio station at Gleiwitz in order to broadcast messages in Polish urging Poles in Silesia to attack Germans. This was followed by actions used to make the attack more convincing, including a Polish prisoner of the Gestapo, Franciszek Honiok, who was dressed in a Polish uniform and killed, before being presented to the press as proof that the attack was the work of Polish saboteurs.	**WW2** – Pearl Harbor **Vietnam** - Gulf of Tonkin **Gulf War 1** - Kuwaiti Babies Tossed from Incubators Downing Street Memo **Global War on Terror** 9-11 False Flag - Best Documentary - Best Book - Best Website **Libya** Libyan Troops raping women on Viagra **Syria** Chemical Weapons Attack on Douma **Iran - 2020** IEDs, Embassy Attack	Shelling of Mainila – This was a false flag incident in which the Soviet Army shelled the Soviet town of Mainila and blamed it on Finland as a Casus Belli to start the Winter War.	

Nazi Germany	US Government Current	Soviet Union/Russia	East Germany

Secret government/real power structure's use of political assassinations of rivals, whistleblowers and dissidents "Free Mason Lyndon Johnson appointed Mason Earl Warren to investigate the death of … John.F. Kennedy. Mason and member of the 33rd degree, Gerald R. Ford, was instrumental in suppressing what little evidence of a conspiratorial nature reached the commission. Responsible for supplying information to the commission was Mason, FBI Director and member of the 33rd degree, J. Edgar Hoover. Former CIA director and Mason Allen Dulles was responsible for most of his agency's data supplied to the panel".- From King Kill 33

		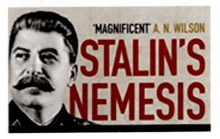	
Yes	**Yes**	**Yes**	**Yes**
Ernst Rohm, night of Long Knives, former Chancellor Kurt von Schleicher and Gustav Ritter von Kahr	**Very Strong Evidence:** John F. Kennedy, Robert Kennedy, Martin Luther King Jr., **Highly Suspected:** Congressman Larry MacDonald, Paul Wellstone, John Kennedy Jr., Vince Foster, Clinton Body Count(CBC Poster), Ron Brown, Gary Webb, Seth Rich, Barry Jennings, Terrance Yeakey, William Colby, Kathy Ferguson, Paul Wilcher, Carlos Ghigliotti, Jerry Luther Parks.	A List of 45+ political assassinations in the Soviet Union and Russia **Modern Russia:** 10 Critics of Vladimir Putin who died in suspicious or violent ways, Zelimkhan Khangoshvili	Swedish journalist Cats Falck and German student Benno Ohnesorg

USA Continued: Jeffrey Epstein, Thomas Bowers (Trump & Epstein's Private Banker), Anthony Bourdain, Barry Seal, Salvatore "Sal" Cincinelli, AK Senator Linda Smith, NYPD Deputy Chief Steven Silks

Nazi Germany	US Government Current	Soviet Union/Russia	East Germany

Political "Temples" dedicated to the State and its deities - In the United States, many government schools, Scout troops, military trainings/postings, veteran's groups, controlled opposition "protests", etc. offer optional low-cost/price-supported trips to Washington D.C./ "Mecca." Impressionable middle school kids/high-school students/scouts/recruits/souldiers are taken into the "cathedral" of the Capital building and the 'temples' along the Potomac and Mall and shown the 'deities' in solemn reverence. They are subtlety conditioned into the hidden religion of Statism.

Yes	**Yes**	**Yes**	**No**
The Ehrentempel were two temples in Munich, constructed by the Nazis in 1935, that housed the sarcophagi of the sixteen members of the party who had been killed in the Beer Hall Putsch, a failed coup attempt. They were later destroyed by the U.S. military during de-nazification.	Lincoln/Jefferson Memorials Monument to Lincoln, a tyrant who has been whitewashed by Statist historians. Lincoln crushed political self-determinism, imprisoned dissenting newspaper editors, conscripted (enslaved) freemen, passed sedition laws, and was one of the first to wage total warfare on civilian populations rather than simply fighting between opposing government armies.	Moscow Palace of Soviets (unfinished) The 1,362 feet (415 m) high palace was to be crowned by a monumental statue of Vladimir Lenin.	

Nazi Germany	US Government Current	Soviet Union/Russia	East Germany

Monopoly Government Fiat Money Steals Value Secretly from the Population - The source of much of organized crime's power is the ability to force the citizenry to use monopoly money, which the government and its agents/allies in banking are allowed to manufacture out of thin air using fractional reserve banking while other forms of currency, like silver and gold, and private cryptocurrencies are banned. This allows the ruling class to buy up and consolidate industry and keeps the population poor by quietly stealing the value of what they earn and save through inflation. Absent the crooked, monopoly money system with a stable currency purchasing power should be going UP each year as innovations and productivity improvements reduce the costs in producing the necessities and luxuries of life.

Yes	**Yes**	**Yes**	**Yes**
Unbacked fiat paper tickets were issued by a private central bank (Reichsbank). Private banks were allowed to create money out of thin air even though the practice is inherently inflationary and steals the value out of everyone else's money.	Unbacked fiat paper tickets are issued by a private central bank (Federal Reserve). Fed-backed banks are allowed to create money out of thin air using fractional reserve banking even though it is inflationary and steals the value of everyone else's money. Citizens' gold coins were stolen through forced conversion in 1933. Silver coins were stolen in 1965 and replaced by base metal tokens.	Unbacked fiat paper tickets were issued by a state-owned central bank (Gosbank). Gosbank was allowed to create money out of thin air even though it is inflationary and steals the value out of everyone else's money.	Worthless outside of East Germany, even in the government's own Intershops, which carried high-quality imported goods they would not accept their own currency.

Nazi Germany	US Government Current	Soviet Union/Russia	East Germany

Spying on Citizens - Organized crime spies on the citizenry to track, trace, and control the population. Political puppets and journalists can be blackmailed. Potential whistle blowers and crisis actors can be monitored. Honest journalists like Michael Hastings, Gary Webb, and Danny Casolaro are often killed when it becomes apparent through surveillance that they are about to expose government criminality.

Yes	Yes	Yes	Yes
The Gestapo employed over 150,000 informants, agents, and accessory personnel. Gestapo agents and informants concentrated on finding suspected political dissidents of the Third Reich. Spying on citizens became pervasive, and the Gestapo encouraged people to turn in "suspect persons" to local authorities.	**The NSA, FBI, and CIA** engage in illegal, unconstitutional, and warrantless wiretapping of the entire population. Much of this was exposed by whistle blowers William Binney & Edward Snowden. No officials have been arrested or charged. Approximately 35,000 people work for the FBI, 21,000 for the CIA, and less than 100,000 for the NSA, but the actual number is classified.	**KGB** – The KGB's successor, the FSB, still publicly monitors all telecommunications under SORM, the government's official surveillance system.

About 490,000 people worked for KGB in 1973. More recent accurate numbers are not available. | **Stasi** – There was one full time agent for every 166 people and one informer for every 6.5 people

When the Berlin Wall fell in 1989, about 189,000 people were informers for the secret police. Over 620,000 people worked undercover for the Stasi in both East and West Germany during the 51 years of the communist state's existence. |

Nazi Germany	US Government Current	Soviet Union/Russia	East Germany

Torture as Policy - Evidence of kakistocracy, rule by the worst scum imaginable, and Statist mind control where cult members will follow any order no matter how immoral and cruel and/or continue to support the "government" when such obvious crimes become known. Known torturer Gina Haspel currently heads CIA.

Yes	**Yes**	**Yes**	**Yes**
Torture techniques included putting people's hands in boiling water until the skin and fingernails came off; pressing a hot poker into their hands; hanging persons by their hands, which were secured behind their backs and then gashing the soles of their feet and making the victims walk on salt; pulling teeth and cutting and twisting off ears.	**Locations:** Abu Ghraib prison, Guantanamo Bay, 9 CIA Black Sites, Homan Square in Chicago **Techniques:** waterboarding (simulated drowning); stress positions; beatings; sexual abuse; Russian roulette; forced nudity, restricted diets; and sleep deprivation, to name a few.	Techniques included: Sleep deprivation for a period of seven to nine days, imposed through constant waking through slaps to the face; beating or striking all sensitive areas of the body with a brass rod or whip, as well as pulling hair from genitals.	Techniques included the burning and mutilation of genitals as well as physical beating. The above image shows a water torture room in the Hohenschönhausen Prison Complex.

Nazi Germany	US Government Current	Soviet Union/Russia	East Germany

Secret Prisons, For-profit prisons (for victimless crimes), Concentration Camps, and "Black Sites" – A clear sign that your "government" is run by organized crime and bad people are secret extra-judicial prisons, concentration camps for ethnic minorities, or For-Profit Prisons where people incarcerated for victimless crimes are forced to work as slave labor for cartel companies.

Yes	**Yes**	**Yes**	**Yes**
An estimated 1200-14,000+ permanent or temporary Concentration Camps, Forced Ghettoization, with some slave labor camps run by specific companies. Auschwitz III was run by IG Farben (Now Bayer/Monsanto)	Camp Delta – Guantanamo Bay, Japanese internment camps during WW2, Homan Square in Chicago, CIA "Black Sites" in a dozen countries, Communications Management Units. Over 500K incarcerated for victimless crimes with some forced to work as slave labor in for-profit prisons.	The Soviet Gulag: 50+ camps and 400+ labor colonies imprisoning 18M+ between 1930-1953 resulting in over 1.5M deaths with many purely political prisoners.	Hohenschönhausen Prison Complex – Where East Germans trying to escape to the west were taken and tortured.

Nazi Germany	US Government Current	Soviet Union/Russia	East Germany
Use of conscription to forcefully enslave people to fight wars and further indoctrinate them into the government's ideology and discipline			
Yes	Yes	Yes	Yes
Forced participation in wars and murderous programs of the State or incarceration.	Forced participation in the wars and murderous program of the State or incarceration.	Forced participation in the wars and murderous program of the State or incarceration.	Forced participation in the wars and murderous program of the State or incarceration.
Manufactured Enemies to unite the population under the government			
Yes	Yes	Yes	Yes
U.S. financial and military industrial complex companies including IBM, Standard Oil, General Motors and Ford supported the Nazis as an excuse to wage war and reap billions in profits.	U.S. support for the Soviet Union was exposed by Antony Sutton in the books: [Wall Street and the Bolshevik Revolution] and [The Best Enemy Money Can Buy]. Major Racey Jordan was a whistle blower who documented that covert support firsthand in [From Major Jordan's Diaries] [Al-Qaeda and ISIS are creations of the US intelligence agencies.]	The Soviets represented the other side of the coin, menacing their own population with the threat of the U.S. to ensure obedience and to transfer wealth from the population to their own military-industrial complex companies.	By extension of their control by the Soviet Union.

Nazi Germany	US Government Current	Soviet Union/Russia	East Germany
Use of paid political violence at the rallies of their political opposition.			
Yes	Yes	No	No
The Sturmabteilung, or "Brown Shirts" were paid political operatives of the National Socialist German Workers Party (similar to US Democratic Party) who were paid to disrupt political rallies of opposition candidates.	The latest example was exposed in October 2016 after investigative reporters with Project Veritas spent a year undercover capturing dozens and dozens of incriminating conversations of engineered violence at Trump rallies, including using the mentally ill and coordination by Hillary Clinton personally.	They seized political power by violence and murder in a scheme financed by organized crime on Wall Street to test and develop stricter slavery than the tax slavery / mafia model of the west.	Enslaved and ruled by the Soviet Union.

"Government"-The Biggest Scam in History Exposed: Propaganda Using Religious Symbolism

www.Government-Scam.com

It's no accident that the MainStreamMedia (the propaganda arm of organized crime) is constantly using trick photography to give the ruler's political puppets the appearance of holiness using religious symbolism. It is one of the many ways the rulers indoctrinate the masses with a pseudo-religion, Statism, slipped to them using government schools, scouting, military and police training, and mainstream media propaganda in news, films, and tell-a-vision "programming".

[_"Government" - The Biggest Scam in History Exposed_](#) is both a book and series of one-page visual overviews of concepts hidden from the public by inter-generational organized crime that has been controlling the flow of information in society. Their "Propaganda Matrix" includes control of the government, government schools, scouting, intelligence agencies, military and police training, and a weaponized media system of 6 companies running hundreds of subsidiaries to give the population the illusion of choice and diversity-of-opinion while propagandizing, deceiving, and distracting us from the reality of our tax slavery and authoritarian control. These [one-pagers](#) are designed to be printed out and shared but with accessible PDF versions with active hypertext links. We have an 8GB Flash Drive/[Dropbox](#) called: _The Liberator_ with additional evidence of government and media criminality.

"Government"-The Biggest Scam in History Exposed: The Religion of Statism

www.Government-Scam.com

Executive Summary

Statism is the belief in the desirability, necessity and legitimacy of a State ("Government") even though there is no iron-clad law of the universe that "government is needed, desirable or legitimate. It is a completely indoctrinated belief system I.E. it has been mandatorily taught to the overwhelming majority of the public through government schools and Private schools where the "government" controls the content of instruction through accreditation, textbook amalgamation and tradition. Statism is a pseudo-religious belief I.E. "Government" is not a physical entity that can be touched. It is a supernatural entity that promises to make the world a better place for the true believers who have accepted the belief system into their world view. The multi-generational organized crime system that has been ruling the planet from behind the scenes uses the same techniques that religions and cults use on their followers to indoctrinate the masses into accepting a ruling class. These techniques include: Religious symbolism in the form of the flag, the Presidency (Pope), "holy documents" in the Constitution and Declaration of Independence, mandatory "church" schools, common prayer where children are required to recite the pledge of allegiance every day at school and at scouting meetings, More common prayer and militarism at sporting events where the government pays teams to propagandize the audience, taking school children on field trips to Washington DC (Mecca) where they are taken to the monuments (temples) to see the Founding Fathers (deities), etc. These techniques produce "citizens" (cult members) willing to hand over ½ their income (tithes) and, in the case of the enforcement class (police) the techniques produce a classic "shaveheaded cult member" willing to kill and cage non-conformists who ignore or violate the laws (commandments) handed down by the Congress/ Courts (church leadership) who sit "above" the citizens and wear robes (vestments). In the case of the military (shave-headed cult members) they are willing to go abroad and kill whom they are told in wars/"police actions" (crusades).

Key Concepts

There is No Such Thing as "Government"
- You can't go to Washington DC and touch "Government"
- It is an idea/belief system that is indoctrinated into kids by gov't schools and most private/parochial schools through accreditation, tradition and textbook amalgamation

The word "Government" literally means "Mind Control" in Latin
- The translation of the original Latin is "To Control the Mind".

The root words are:
- **Gubenare** – Control, Govern, Rule
- **Mens/Mente** – Mind

The belief in "Government" is mandatorily indoctrinated into the masses
- No one is born believing that handing over ½ your income in overt taxes, covert taxes, and inflation to a ruling class is a good idea
- Human beings are free, sentient beings who don't owe their allegiance/income to anyone just because they were born on one side or another of an imaginary line.
- Mandatory "free" government K-12 schools & accredited private schools spend ~12,000 hours indoctrinating and legitimizing this belief system in a hidden curriculum
- The belief is reinforced through government institutions, government, police/military training, scouting (pre-military training & flag worship), paid-for militarism/statism at sporting events and a propaganda system where 6 companies running hundreds of subsidiaries give the illusion of choice but are controlling the information the masses receive to limit their knowledge and secretly reinforcing the status quo and "legitimacy" of the system in movies, television shows, magazines, etc.

The government schools use classical "cult indoctrination" techniques on kids
- Most government teachers/administrators are ignorant/willfully ignorant of the hidden curriculum and brainwashed themselves and don't know/refuse to research the history of the Prussian education system and its creators own admissions that the system was designed to control the masses and instill obedience to authority:
  - **Indoctrination Techniques include:**
    - Common Prayer: The pledge of allegiance at school and national anthem at sporting events
    - Civics and social studies that teach kids the Statist world view
    - Focus on learning about the Presidents (Popes) and legitimacy of Gov't
    - Socialization of the enforcement class (police) through D.A.R.E. program
    - Promotion of military, selective service, and military recruiters in schools
  - **Obedience Techniques include:**
    - The inability to leave or even go to the bathroom without permission
    - Public shaming (Red, Yellow, Green) and collective punishment
    - Responding to Pavlovian bells, walking in line, obedience to police, etc.

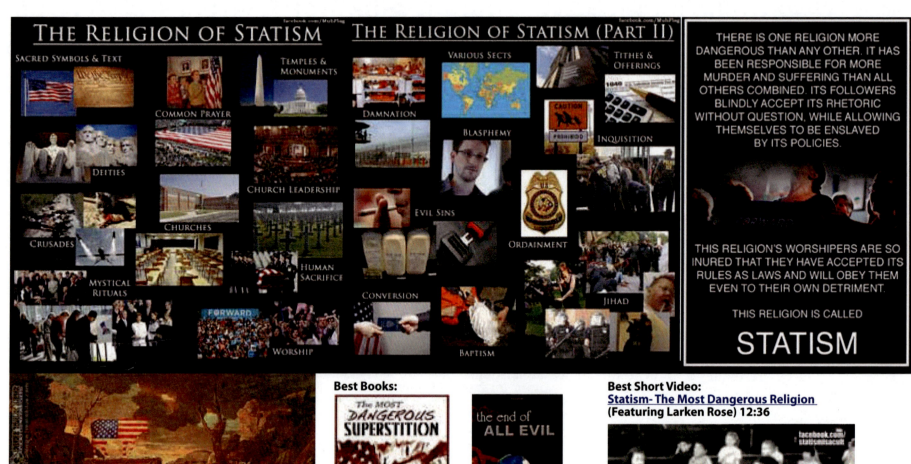

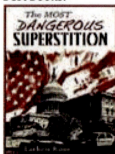

Best Books:

The Most Dangerous Superstition
by Larken Rose

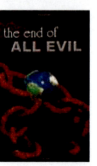

The End of All Evil
By Jeremy Locke

Best Short Video:
Statism- The Most Dangerous Religion
(Featuring Larken Rose) 12:36

"Government" - The Biggest Scam in History Exposed is both a book and series of one-page visual overviews of concepts hidden from the public by inter-generational organized crime that has been controlling the flow of information in society. Their "Propaganda Matrix" includes control of the government, government schools, scouting, intelligence agencies, military and police training, and a weaponized media system of 6 companies running hundreds of subsidiaries to give the population the illusion of choice and diversity-of-opinion while propagandizing, deceiving, and distracting us from the reality of our tax slavery and authoritarian control. These one-pagers are designed to be printed out and shared but with accessible PDF versions with active hypertext links. We have an 8GB Flash Drive/Dropbox called: *The Liberator* with additional evidence of government and media criminality.

"Government"-The Biggest Scam in History Exposed: The Shady History of the Constitution

www.Government-Scam.com

Executive Summary

It is frankly absurd on its face that any written document or political ritual like voting can grant one group of men the ability to rule and control another group of men, delegate rights they don't have personally to a "government" or that succeeding generations can be bound by a contract that none of them or even their forbears signed. For those who remain religiously attached to the "holy document" of the Constitution or believe themselves bound by an oath they were tricked (fraudulent inducement), forced, or paid to take then here are some facts that support our thesis that organized crime interests have been using "Government" and control of the media to rob and control the population since the very creation of the Constitution.

The creation and ratification of the Constitution is not what most government school children have been led to believe. It wasn't designed to protect life, liberty, and property and limit government as claimed and its failure in those aspects or even its inability to ensure the most basic of freedoms specified in the Bill of Rights is evidence of its failure as a protection from tyranny and its success as a means of enslaving, controlling and robbing the population.

The real story of the Constitution is a "Wall Street (of the time)" **conspiracy**, and that is the *exact term* that many of their contemporaries used to describe what had occurred, to create a system that would allow moneyed interests represented by political puppets to tax everyone on the continent for their benefit and control commerce and the currency which they started doing immediately after ratification.

The conspirators were led by slave-owning Freemasons James Madison and John Jay and suspected freemason and slave owner Alexander Hamilton. They hijacked a convention **convened only to revise the existing Articles of Confederation between the States** and, **after almost half the delegates refused to participate, wouldn't sign and/or left early** produced an unauthorized replacement giving unprecedented control to a Federal government that would be controlled by the exact participants in the years to come. In short order they used this new government to begin taxing the population to pay off "Wall Street" speculators who had bought up Revolutionary War bonds from veterans and businesses that had accepted them during the war, for pennies on the dollar. Hamilton, as first secretary of the treasury, paid these speculators 100% of the face value. He then went on to pay off the war debts of the individual states who had never paid them (esp. Mass.) at the expense of those who had (Virginia). Thomas Jefferson openly questioned the validity of these debts and amounts. After Pennsylvania farmers began to rebel against a progressive tax on Whiskey that hit the poor hardest and benefited large distillers like George Washington, Washington and Hamilton led an Army of 13,000 into Pennsylvania to force compliance with the tax by rousting citizens out of bed into the snow, searching homes without warrants, and forcing citizens to sign oaths of loyalty to the federal government.

Key Concepts

Absent a 12,000 hour indoctrination program run by the government and the on-going propaganda of bought-and-paid-for media, it is absurd to believe that a couple of dozen slave owners on a continent of three million people can write down on a fancy piece of paper that they run everything, then have their newspapers proclaim it valid but that seems to be exactly what happened.

"That investigation into the nature and construction of the new constitution, which the conspirators have so long and zealously struggled against, has, notwithstanding their partial success, so far taken place as to ascertain the enormity of their criminality. That system which was pompously displayed as the perfection of government, proves upon examination to be the most odious system of tyranny that was ever projected, a many headed hydra of despotism, whose complicated and various evils would be infinitely more oppressive and afflictive than the scourge of any single tyrant: the objects of dominion would be tortured to gratify the calls of ambition and cravings of power, of rival despots contending for the sceptre of superiority; the devoted people would experience a distraction of misery"

– Anti-Federalist Samuel Bryan writing as Centinel in Centinel XII Jan 23rd 1788

The History and Facts the "Government" School Leaves Out

The delegates assembled in Philadelphia in May 1787 for the purpose of amending, **not replacing**, the Articles of Confederation were very different from the revolutionaries that signed the Declaration of Independence in 1776. The famous revolutionaries were not present: Jefferson and Adams were in Europe, Thomas Paine, Sam Adams, and Chris Gadsden were not chosen and Patrick Henry refused to participate outright claiming he "smelt a rat". Out of the 74 delegates chosen 19 refused or didn't attend!

Out of the 55 delegates who showed up 41 were politicians, 34 were lawyers, 11 were admitted freemasons (with 2 additional that would join lodges after the convention) with over a dozen more suspected. According to Maryland Delegate James McHenry, at least 21 of the 55 delegates favored some form of monarchy.

The convention operated under great secrecy: Held in the summer months with all the windows nailed shut, sentries posted at the door, and all the participants sworn to secrecy. The proceedings wouldn't be published for 32 years later. Madison's edited notes 53 years later.

It's unlikely that the States would have sent delegates at all if they had known of the conspirators' plans to abolish the articles and replace them with a Federal government and many delegates openly protested. William Patterson echoed many: "We ought to keep within its limits or be charged by our constituents with usurpation... We have no power to go beyond the confederation... If the confederacy is wrong then let us return to our States and obtain larger powers, not assume them ourselves."

Of the **74** delegates appointed, **19** refused outright or didn't attend, **14** left early some in open disgust, of the **41** who stayed through September three refused to sign, leaving **38** out of 74 (53% hardly a plurality) and they signed not as delegates but "In Witness Whereof".

Of the **38** who "gave themselves the power to make up rules for everyone and take the wealth of others" **80% would personally enrich themselves by holding some office under the Constitution** including 2 Presidents, 1 Vice President, 5 Justices, 11 Senators, and 8 Representatives.

Control of the Perception – Evident then as evident today

Similar to organized crime's control of the media today, the "Wall Street" crowd were controlling information/perception during the ratification debates. According to Van Doren's *The Great Rehearsal*, Anti-Federalist speeches were never printed because the convention's transcriber, Thomas Lloyd, "appears to have been bought off by the Federalists, and published only...speeches by Federalists Wilson and McKean". Serious allegations were made in New York and elsewhere of Federalist mail-tampering. The Pennsylvania Herald, the only paper reporting on the ratification debates was bought off as described:

"The authors and abettors of the new constitution shudder at the term conspirators being applied to them, as it designates their true character... Attempts to prevent discussion by shackling the press ought ever to be a signal of alarm to freemen, and considered as an annunciation of meditated tyranny... ***when every means failed to shackle the press, the free and independent papers were attempted to be demolished by withdrawing all the subscriptions to them within the sphere of the influence of the conspirators...The Pennsylvania Herald has been silenced... the editor is dismissed and the debates of the convention thereby suppressed.***"* – Centinel XII, Jan 23rd 1788

Best Book: Hologram of Liberty – The Constitutions Shocking Alliance with Big Government **By Kenneth W Royce**

Hologram of Liberty explains the Anti-Federalist case and the evidence for the conspiracy of wealthy speculators, lawyers, and politicians to impose a one-sided contract to control and tax the population in a scheme that personally enriched themselves. This summary borrows liberally from Royce's work and other scholars.

"Government" - The Biggest Scam in History Exposed is both a book and series of one-page visual overviews of concepts hidden from the public by inter-generational organized crime that has been controlling the flow of information in society. Their "Propaganda Matrix" includes control of the government, "public" schools, scouting, intelligence agencies, military and police training, and a weaponized media system of 6 companies running hundreds of subsidiaries to give the population the illusion of choice and diversity-of-opinion while propagandizing, deceiving, and distracting us from the reality of our tax slavery and authoritarian control. These one-pagers are designed to be printed out and shared but with accessible PDF versions with active hypertext links. We have an 8GB Flash Drive/Dropbox called: *The Liberator* with additional evidence of government and media criminality.

"Government"-The Biggest Scam in History Exposed: The Shady History of the Pledge of Allegiance

www.Government-Scam.com

Executive Summary

The massive five story Youth's Companion Building, built in 1892 and known locally in Boston as the "Pledge of Allegiance Building", still stands today and gives an idea of the size and scope of the operation.

The original pledge of allegiance was a media creation of avowed national socialists and free masons running a well-financed publishing company targeting kids in the late 19th century. The company was the Perry Mason Company and they published the most popular magazine of the time called The Youth's Companion. The magazine's circulation hit over 500,000 in 1897 and pushed a nationalist socialist/military socialism agenda. The pledge of allegiance was attributed to staff writer and freemason Francis Bellamy while the socialist "Bellamy Salute", which came to be used by other nationalist socialist regimes including Adolf Hitler is credited to junior partner, editor and fellow freemason James Upham who also assigned the writing of the pledge to Bellamy. Francis Bellamy's cousin Edward Bellamy, son of a freemason, was the author of an 1888 international best seller advocating military socialism called Looking Backward from 2000 to 1887 frequently cited as "the Bible of National Socialism". The Bellamy's were unapologetic in their advocation of National Socialism and Military Socialism, mandatory government schools, militarism and used their magazine to begin popularizing a national "Pledge of Allegiance", which they first published in 1892 with a premium program designed to promote, sell and distribute the Federal US Flag into local schools where it had not been used or present before, which contributed to the federal takeover of the individual states and the average person's religious attachment to an artificially indoctrinated holy symbol.

Key Concepts

Most Americans are familiar with the infamous "Heil Hitler/Nazi Salute" pictured here being taught to children by government teachers in Nazi Germany, but are unaware that the salute originated in the United States where it was used for over three decades prior (1892-1926) to the Nazi's adoption in our mandatory government school system. **The pledge and salute were used to forcefully indoctrinate our population into the ideas of national socialism and military socialism that have supplanted the supposedly original intent of limited government and freedom that US schools still pretend exists.**

National Socialism with its taxation, militarism, robotic saluting, federal control, mandatory schools running the Prussian model of education, and history of tyranny was and remains antithetical to the freedom supposedly enshrined in "The Constitution".

The pledge of allegiance is forced on students in mandatory government schools from pre-school and Kindergarten before the children are old enough to comprehend the ideas to which they are pledging their allegiance which is, in and of itself, unethically manipulative.

While the original Bellamy Salute featured the upturned hand, in practice school children simply stuck out their hands and face down became the norm and is the version that is visible in the majority of surviving photographs from the time with the noted exception of a series taken by Hollywood's L.A. Times in 1942/1943 around the time of the changeover to the hand-over-the-heart. The professionally lit classroom scene on the cover of this book and others appear to be a coordinated attempt to distance the pledge from the then obvious crimes of the German Socialists by returning to the original Bellamy version with upturned palm proving that the difference between socialism and fascism is just a matter of degree.

Resources to Learn More

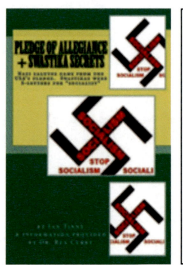

"At a signal from the Principal the pupils, in ordered ranks, hands to the side, face the Flag. Another signal is given; every pupil gives the flag the military salute -- right hand lifted, palm downward, to align with the forehead and close to it. Standing thus, all repeat together, slowly, "I pledge allegiance to my Flag and the Republic for which it stands; one Nation indivisible, with Liberty and Justice for all." At the words, "to my Flag," the right hand is extended gracefully, palm upward, toward the Flag, and remains in this gesture till the end of the affirmation; whereupon all hands immediately drop to the side." - From The Youth's Companion, 65 (1892): 446–447.

Best Short Video:
Bellamy Salute is American Nazism From Pledge to Flag

The video features clips from the 1925 movie The Vanishing American showing American Indian children being indoctrinated into the artificial religion of Statism in a mandatory government school by a white teacher. The scene demonstrates that once organized crime conquered the Indians and stole their land they used the Prussian model of education in mandatory Indian Boarding Schools where children were separated from their families to turn the once proud and free native Americans into "tax payers" and "order followers". The film makes a hero out of Nophaie, a tribal leader who provides horses for the US Army and gets other Indians to enlist and fight in World War 1, a foreign war. This dynamic illustrates the original Etienne de la Boetie's observation that, once conquered, most (but not all) can be made to adopt the habits and customs of their enslavers.

Best Book:
Pledge of Allegiance & Swastika Secrets: Nazism in the USA from Francis Bellamy & Edward Bellamy
By Dr. Rex Curry and Ian Tinney

In addition to exposing the history of the socialist Pledge of Allegiance, the book documents how the Swastika was adopted and rotated in Nazi Germany to symbolize the "S" of Socialism. Socialism, communism and other forms of collectivism are tools used by organized crime to control/"chump" large segments of the population with the promise of money stolen from others.

In practice the majority of US students just stuck out their hands and recited the pledge with "palms down". Hollywood begins glamorizing the salute in 1907's Ben Hur and it is adopted by Italian fascists (1919) and then the National Socialist German Workers (Nazi) Party in 1926 and the German Army in 1944.

"Government" - The Biggest Scam in History Exposed is both a book and series of one-page visual overviews of concepts hidden from the public by inter-generational organized crime that has been controlling the flow of information in society. Their "Propaganda Matrix" includes control of the government, "public" schools, scouting, intelligence agencies, military and police training, and a weaponized media system of 6 companies running hundreds of subsidiaries to give the population the illusion of choice and diversity-of-opinion while propagandizing, deceiving, and distracting us from the reality of our tax slavery and authoritarian control. These one-pagers are designed to be printed out and shared but with accessible PDF versions with active hypertext links. We have an 8GB Flash Drive/Dropbox called: The Liberator with additional evidence of government and media criminality.

"Government"-The Biggest Scam in History Exposed: Public (Government) School Indoctrination
www.Government-Scam.com

Executive Summary

The American school system, directly modeled after the 19th century Prussian approach, is rooted heavily in control, obedience, and indoctrination.

By glorifying collectivism and authority, public (government) schools prime children to tacitly accept subsequent authoritarianism from all realms of government and military. From monopolizing students' time and demanding they ask permission for basic human functions — like going to the bathroom — to imposing one-size-fits all teaching approaches, submission and conformity are constantly promoted.

Students are indoctrinated into the pseudo-religion of statism using the same techniques employed by other cults: for example, pledges/oaths, holy documents, trips to D.C. to see the temples/deities. Selectively presented snippets of history support these myths, imbuing students with an unshakable faith in the government's universality, inevitability, and righteousness. Militarism and nationalism pervade the system through junior training programs like ROTC, and the state's legitimacy is never questioned or debated.

Other methods of control permeate the system. In recent years, the pharmaceutical industry has benefitted from the increase in diagnoses of ADD and ADHD in children, which is largely due to children's inability to conform to schools' rigid standards of control. These drugs, as well as mandatory vaccines, directly affect students' body chemistry. So do the vast supplies of genetically modified, pesticide-ridden foods provided by state-empowered conglomerations.

Because of these hidden methods of control and modern consequences of rampant statism, public schooling is ground zero for producing obedient statist subjects and order followers willing to kill on command.

Key Concepts

Obedience to the government, police and authority figures is lesson #1
- Assigned seating imposes constant, uniform control over student movement
- Drill bells dictate where and when students may move during the course of the day
- Students are usually required to collectively stand and pledge allegiance to the flag, which continues with the additional "common prayer" of the anthem at sporting events
- If students are late or do not adhere to other standards, they face punitive measures, including public shaming and Red/Yellow/Green troublemaker boards
- On the other side of the coin, students are often forced to face collective punishment for the actions of a single student
- Police are increasingly present in schools, patrolling campuses and enforcing security checks with metal detectors and conducting random searches of students' private property, reinforcing the notion that school is a prison — and everyone must submit to government (organized crime) control from an early age.

Indoctrination into the hidden religion of Statism is "Education"
- Students are expected to pledge allegiance to an artificial religious symbol in a kind of "common prayer" on a daily basis from K-12
- They are taught that gov't is both legitimate, necessary and desirable without ever examining those premises or the immorality of the concept.
- Young students learn of the mythology of the "Founding Fathers", "social contract", the holy documents of the Constitution/BoRs, the justifications for the gov'ts murderous wars, and that stealing is OK when gov't does it!
- What is left out of these lessons is equally important, from the CIA's covert, undemocratic operations to the Federal Reserve and the real reasons for war
- Whether it is history, civics, or any other subject, teaching methods usually require memorization, regurgitation, and often, standardized, multiple choice testing methods that crush independent thought and promote obedience.

Chemical Control
- Thanks to propagandized obedience and state-sanctioned influence of the pharmaceutical industry and food industry, children are pumped full of chemicals, from ADD and ADHD drugs and mercury and aluminum-laced vaccines to toxic processed food with genetically modified (GMO) ingredients, sugar, glutamates, glyphosate, refined grains, rBGH, BPA/BPS, soy, and fluoridated water.
- Classic indoctrination methods, combined with a fetish for submission and the modern American government-sponsored corporatocracy, create docile Statist children, some of whom ultimately shave their heads and become "order followers".

Resources to Learn More

Best Short Videos:

The American Way? Our Connection to Nazi Germany
Produced by The School Sucks Project
https://www.youtube.com/watch?v=okPnDZ1Txlo

Best Books:

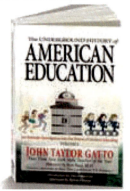

[The Underground History of American Education](#)
- John Taylor Gatto

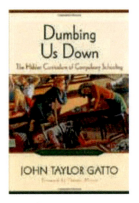

[Dumbing us Down – The Hidden Curriculum of Compulsory Schooling](#)
– John Taylor Gatto

[The Deliberate Dumbing Down of America](#)
– Charlotte Iserbyt

John Taylor Gatto – Radio Interview
https://youtu.be/m2ItZzcHd4M?t=27s

Could the real goal of mandatory government education be shave-headed cult members / "order followers" willing to kill foreigners and enforce orders from the leaders of an artificially indoctrinated Statist religion? Is this why classic, textbook cult indoctrination techniques including Pavlovian bells, pledges/oaths, flags/artificial holy symbols, collective punishment, public shaming, Scouting/jROTC "uniforms" and others are being used in schools?

"It is worthy of remark that a belief constantly inculcated during the early years of life, whilst the brain is impressible, appears to acquire almost the nature of an instinct; and the very essence of an instinct is that it is followed independently of reason."—Charles Darwin, The Descent of Man, 1871

[*"Government" - The Biggest Scam in History Exposed*](#) is both a book and series of one-page visual overviews of concepts hidden from the public by inter-generational organized crime that has been controlling the flow of information in society. Their "Propaganda Matrix" includes control of the government, "public" schools, scouting, intelligence agencies, military and police training, and a weaponized media system of 6 companies running hundreds of subsidiaries to give the population the illusion of choice and diversity-of-opinion while propagandizing, deceiving, and distracting us from the reality of our tax slavery and authoritarian control. These [one-pagers](#) are designed to be printed out and shared but with accessible PDF versions with active hypertext links. We have an 8GB Flash Drive/[Dropbox](#) called: [*The Liberator*](#) with additional evidence of government and media criminality.

"Government"-The Biggest Scam in History Exposed:
The Private Federal Reserve and Theft of Fractional Reserve Banking
www.Government-Scam.com

Executive Summary

In 1913 organized crime banking interests lobbied and bribed Congress to pass the Federal Reserve Act which created the private Federal Reserve (FED) to back-stop and "legalize" the ability of private banks to create money out of thin air and lend it at interest. The process is called fractional reserve banking and the basics of the swindle is that when you go to the bank to get a mortgage the bank is not lending you another depositor's money. They simply create the money with a few strokes on the keyboard and the average person spends the rest of their life paying interest on a loan created out of thin air. If a bank gets in financial trouble and/or experiences a "run-on-the-bank" where depositors begin to pull their money then the FED steps in and provides the troubled bank(s) unlimited capital to maintain faith in the crooked system.

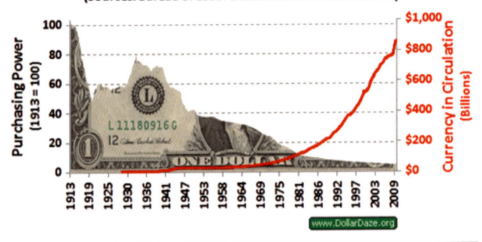

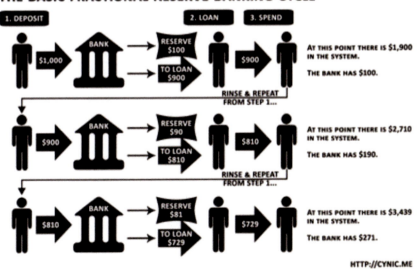

The Theft of Inflation

In addition to the inherent unfairness of allowing certain companies (banks) the monopoly privilege of creating money, the process steals the purchasing power from the dollars earned and saved by everyone else in society. As the banks create more and more dollars the excess dollars begin to compete with the existing dollars in the market and bid up prices and simultaneously reduce the purchasing power of existing dollars in circulation. This is the main reason why the cost of almost everything in the economy (housing, healthcare, education, energy, etc.) is going UP when, absent the organized crime money system, costs should be going DOWN as innovations and productivity improvements reduce the costs associated with producing the necessities and luxuries of everyday life. Not only is society being robbed by the inflationary theft of rising prices but it is being robbed of the reduced costs and growing purchasing power that would exist absent the organized crime banking system. Absent the anomalies of hot housing markets and hot stocks, it isn't that the value of your home and portfolio are rising, it now simply takes more rapidly depreciating dollars to buy the same amount of housing and stocks.

Table S1: Top 50 control-holders. Shareholders are ranked by network control (according to threshold model, TM). Column indicate country, NACE industrial sector code, actor's position in the bow-tie sections, cumulative network control. Notice that NACE code starting with 65 belong to the financial sector.

Rank	Economic actor name	Country	NACE code	Network position	Cumul. net control (TM)
1	BARCLAYS PLC	GB	6512	SCC	4.05
2	CAPITAL GROUP COMPANIES INC, THE	US	6713	IN	6.66
3	FMR CORP	US	6713	IN	8.94
4	AXA	FR	6712	SCC	11.21
5	STATE STREET CORPORATION	US	6713	SCC	13.02
6	JPMORGAN CHASE & CO.	US	6512	SCC	14.55
7	LEGAL & GENERAL GROUP PLC	GB	6603	SCC	16.02
8	VANGUARD GROUP, INC., THE	US	7415	IN	17.25
9	UBS AG	CH	6512	SCC	18.46
10	MERRILL LYNCH & CO., INC.	US	6712	SCC	19.45
11	WELLINGTON MANAGEMENT CO. L.L.P.	US	6713	IN	20.33
12	DEUTSCHE BANK AG	DE	6512	SCC	21.17
13	FRANKLIN RESOURCES, INC.	US	6512	SCC	21.99
14	CREDIT SUISSE GROUP	CH	6512	SCC	22.81
15	WALTON ENTERPRISES LLC	US	2923	T&T	23.56
16	BANK OF NEW YORK MELLON CORP.	US	6512	IN	24.28
17	NATIXIS	FR	6512	SCC	24.98
18	GOLDMAN SACHS GROUP, INC., THE	US	6712	SCC	25.64
19	T. ROWE PRICE GROUP, INC.	US	6713	SCC	26.29
20	LEGG MASON, INC.	US	6712	SCC	26.92
21	MORGAN STANLEY	US	6712	SCC	27.56
22	MITSUBISHI UFJ FINANCIAL GROUP, INC.	JP	6512	SCC	28.16

The list above comes from a 2011 study called The Network of Global Corporate Control, which analyzed 37 million global companies and 43,060 transnational corporations and built a model of who owns and controls what and discovered that just **147 firms**, primarily banks and financial institutions control **40% of global wealth**.

The Results: Monopoly

Imagine you are playing the game Monopoly with a group of people where the banker is cheating and giving himself unlimited funds. At the end of the game who owns everything on the board and who are renters and debtors? The ability to create money out of thin air has enabled the banks to:

1. Buy, consolidate, and weaponize the media into nothing but deception and distraction.

2. Provide unlimited funds to a small handful of organized crime companies to consolidate their own industries and trade as a cartel. See our Liberator folder on Banking Cartel's Monopoly Consolidation.

"Government" - The Biggest Scam in History Exposed is both a book and series of one-page visual overviews of concepts hidden from the public by inter-generational organized crime that has been controlling the flow of information in society. Their "Propaganda Matrix" includes control of the government, "public" schools, scouting, intelligence agencies, military and police training, and a weaponized media system of 6 companies running hundreds of subsidiaries to give the population the illusion of choice and diversity-of-opinion while propagandizing, deceiving, and distracting us from the reality of our tax slavery and authoritarian control. These one-pagers are designed to be printed out and shared but with accessible PDF versions with active hypertext links. We have an 8GB Flash Drive/Dropbox called: The Liberator with additional evidence of government and media criminality.

"Government"-The Biggest Scam in History Exposed: The Propaganda Matrix

www.Government-Scam.com

The most powerful weapon on the planet is control of perception and it is a "binary" weapon made up of hundreds of companies, government agencies and organizations that give the population their information to create and control their "cult-ure". Cult-ure is the dominant belief system and the root word is "cult" which is why police/ judges/ bailiffs/ sheriffs/ prosecutors/ prison guards and "soul-diers" and other "order followers" can't be reasoned with. Plato tells this story in his Allegory of the Cave where prisoners were chained facing the wall of a deep cave. Behind the prisoners was a walkway and behind the walkway a fire. Puppeteers crossed the walkway holding objects that cast shadows on the wall. The "shadow play" became the prisoner's life and even when one prisoner escaped to see the reality of the world he was unable to explain that reality to his former friends because they had no frame of reference because all they ever knew was the shadow play. Organized crime governments have used this system to convince their populations that the world is a certain way and it is everyone's duty to turn over 50% of their income in overt/covert taxes while using the theft of inflation, military procurement fraud, no-bid contracts, government-granted monopolies and dozens of other invisible means of economic warfare against them. This allows organized crime to steal trillions and easily spend hundreds of billions a year controlling every screen and distracting/deceiving every audience.

Obscene criminal profits are generated in many ways: the theft of taxes which are laundered through the governments to the organized crime "slave owners" through their monopoly banking/oil/pharma/military-industrial-complex companies. Interest on the national debt, "bailouts", and free money from fractional reserve banking for Big Banking, mandatory mercury and aluminum-laced vaccines for Big Pharma, ethanol and agricultural subsidies for Big Ag, unneeded military spending benefits the big military-industrial-intelligence complex who continually menace the population with staged wars and false-flag terrorism. The fact that the world is self-organizing, both political parties are run by the same criminal interests, and that there is no need for "governments" and the force and violence they employ are ideas that are never presented to the tax slaves... on any channel... until now...

My favorite analogy about the LameStreamMedia is that the former Soviet Union was a very poor country. They could only afford 2 state propaganda organs: Pravda and Izvestia. In Russian Pravda means "Truth" and Izvestia is loosely translated as "The News". The running joke in the Soviet Union was: "There is no truth in Pravda and there is no news in Izvestia". We are/were a very wealthy country... We have 6 major propaganda organs. The organized crime oligarchy that controls the country and much of the planet has been using their complete control of virtually everything that the average person sees on a given day to weave an artificially-created reality with regard to politics/economics/history/current events when they are not distracting us with sports & mindless entertainment, corrupting our morals, predictively programming us, or other propaganda crimes.

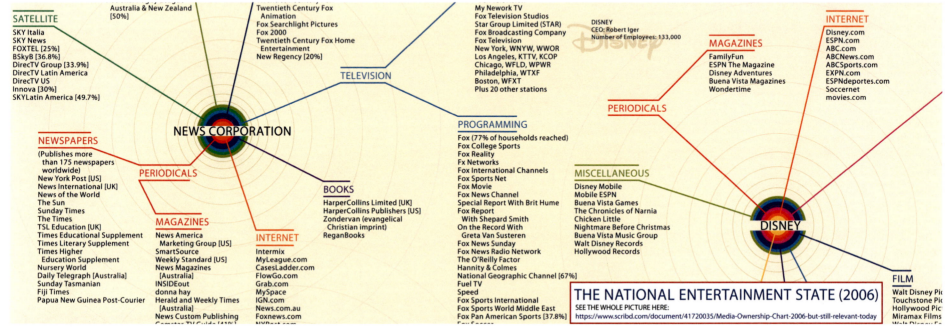

"*Deception becomes more difficult as the number of channels of information available to the target increases. However, within limits, the greater the number of controlled channels the greater the likelihood the deception will be believed.*" – Deception Maxims: Fact & Folklore – CIA Deception Research Program Paper – June 1981

The main identifiable vehicles for creating/managing/controlling the content of MainStreamMedia are Bilderberg Group, Trilateral Commission and Council on Foreign Relations (CFR) control of the Media and the CIA's control of key journalists that was made public during the Church Committee hearings in 1975 where it was disclosed that the CIA had hundreds of journalists on the payroll. A quote from the commission: *"The CIA currently maintains a network of several hundred foreign individuals around the world who provide intelligence for the CIA and at times attempt to influence opinion through the use of covert propaganda. These individuals provide the CIA with direct access to a large number of newspapers and periodicals, scores of press services and news agencies, radio and television stations, commercial book publishers, and other foreign media outlets."*

"Government" - The Biggest Scam in History Exposed is both a book and series of one-page visual overviews of concepts hidden from the public by inter-generational organized crime that has been controlling the flow of information in society. Their "Propaganda Matrix" includes control of the government, "public" schools, scouting, intelligence agencies, military and police training, and a weaponized media system of 6 companies running hundreds of subsidiaries to give the population the illusion of choice and diversity-of-opinion while propagandizing, deceiving, and distracting us from the reality of our tax slavery and authoritarian control. These one-pagers are designed to be printed out and shared but with accessible PDF versions with active hypertext links. We have an 8GB Flash Drive/Dropbox called: *The Liberator* with additional evidence of government and media criminality.

"Government"-The Biggest Scam in History Exposed:
Control of the media and, by extension, human perception
www.Government-Scam.com

Executive Summary

"If there was really an organized crime conspiracy to enslave the population then surely someone would have reported on it in the media"

In our one-pager: The Propaganda Matrix we feature a media ownership chart showing how six media companies running hundreds of subsidiaries give the population the illusion of choice and diversity-of-opinion. While that visualization illustrates the ownership structure of the media including movies, television, book, and magazine publishers, theatres, and theme parks, it doesn't explain how individual reporters, editors, and publishers are given their "marching orders" to widely cover up Government criminality and propagandize the public across hundreds of media platforms.

If you want to rob the world, you have to have meetings! - In this one-pager we feature visualizations from Swiss Propaganda Research showing how just three organizations: The Bilderberg Group, the Council on Foreign Relations, and the Trilateral Commission are able to coordinate the activities of hundreds of publishers, editors and journalists. I am not suggesting that every person receives specific instructions, even though prominent journalists including Udo Ulfkotte have admitted to publishing stories written by the CIA under his name and the L.A. Times' Ken Dilanian who was outed as a CIA tool through an agency FOIA request.

Most honest journalists are fired (or even killed as was San Jose Mercury News reporter Gary Webb, Rolling Stone's Michael Hastings, or Danny Casolaro) whenever they try to report on forbidden topics: CIA drug running, 9-11 Truth, the massacre and subsequent cover up of 80 men, women, and children in Waco, the criminality of fractional reserve banking and Federal Reserve policy. Intelligent and immoral publishers, editors, and reporters like Bilderberg "journalists" Fareed Zakaria and George Stephanopoulos can easily get themselves on the gravy train of six, seven or even eight figure salaries by not just covering up the corruption, but taking leadership positions in creating and disseminating propaganda that supports our manufactured and unnecessary multi-trillion dollar wars and the mass theft of trillions through "bailouts" and inflation. The key concept to understand is that if organized crime is stealing **trillions** of dollars through fractional reserve banking, unnecessary military spending, bank "bailouts" and other criminality then it is easy and cost-effective for them to spend a couple of hundred billion a year to buy up and control the media. Almost every single channel, almost every single publication including the couple of hundred people who are paid/allowed to talk "politics" and current events on the weaponized tell-lie-vision are controlled.

Visualizations

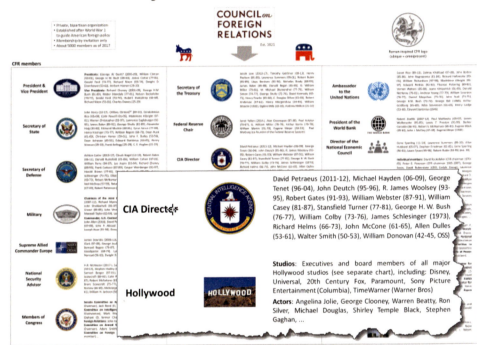

Get the expanded, high resolution version from The Liberator:
https://www.dropbox.com/s/pyebndx0es9cupp/cfr-imperial-council-hdv.png?dl=0

This 2017 chart shows how one organization, The Council on Foreign Relations (CFR), has infiltrated and promoted its membership into the key positions of media, entertainment, politics, banking, diplomacy, the military, think tanks, NGOs, universities, and the intelligence agencies for decades through both "Democrat" and "Republican" administrations. The link below is to a 2010 chart from the Fund to Restore an Educated Electorate showing the multi-generational dominance of the CFR, Bilderberg Group, and Trilateral Commission:

https://www.dropbox.com/s/hxjuhgtwkqd15aw/2010%20Bilderberg%20CFR%20Trilateral%20Chart.pdf?dl=0

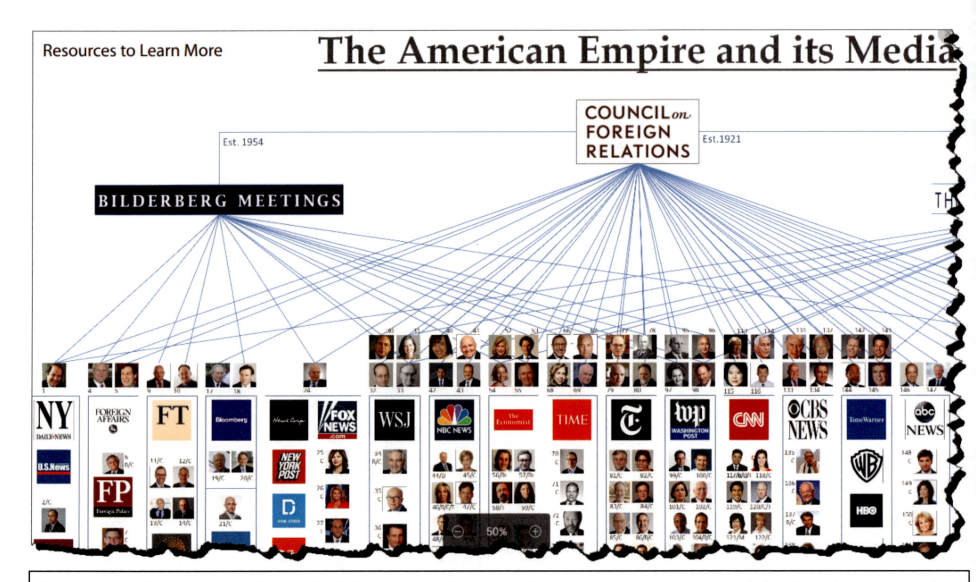

The American Empire and It's Media – V1.0 2017 by Swiss Propaganda Research – Get the entire, expanded high resolution version from *The Liberator*: https://www.dropbox.com/s/w02s4twyog3whng/cfr-bilderberg-media-network-hdv-spr.png?dl=0

"Government" - The Biggest Scam in History Exposed is both a book and series of one-page visual overviews of concepts hidden from the public by inter-generational organized crime that has been controlling the flow of information in society. Their "Propaganda Matrix" includes control of the government, "public" schools, scouting, intelligence agencies, military and police training, and a weaponized media system of 6 companies running hundreds of subsidiaries to give the population the illusion of choice and diversity-of-opinion while propagandizing, deceiving, and distracting us from the reality of our tax slavery and authoritarian control. These one-pagers are designed to be printed out and shared, but with accessible PDF versions with active hypertext links. We have an 8GB Flash Drive/Dropbox called: *The Liberator* with additional evidence of government and media criminality.

"Government"-The Biggest Scam in History Exposed: Organized Crime's Front Groups & Secret Societies

www.Government-Scam.com

Executive Summary

"If you want to rob the world then you have to have meetings." – EdlB2

In our one-pager: Control of the Media we featured two 2017 charts showing how just three organizations, the Council on Foreign Relations, the Bilderberg Group, and the Trilateral Commission include in their membership the key publishers, editors, and journalists at essentially every major network, wire service, Hollywood studio, newspaper of record, internet publication, and other sources of "news" and cult-ure creation. Convicted pedophile and apparent Mossad asset Jeffrey Epstein was a member of all three groups and running an apparent blackmail operation on politicians and prominent individuals as another method of control.

The 2010 chart on the back of this page shows how that control extends to everything from the Presidency, Congress, Judicial, IMF, CIA, FBI and other key positions of power. Here is a short primer on each of these organizations plus others where organized crime recruits, trains, organizes, and gets their membership together for meetings. Just because someone is a member of these organizations doesn't make them a criminal. Many are recruited and found too honest/moral for the higher levels of the program or are dupes used as window dressing I.E. "Porch Masons". Some organization's members also undergo classic, unethically manipulative cult indoctrination techniques to assure their conformity to the required control/secrecy.

The Council on Foreign Relations - "The Council on Foreign Relations is the American branch of a society which organized in England ... (and) ... believes national boundaries should be obliterated and one world rule established." [With No Apologies by Senator Barry Goldwater, P. 126

The Trilateral Commission was formed in 1973 by private citizens of Japan, Europe (European Union countries), and North America (United States and Canada) to foster closer cooperation among these core democratic industrialized areas of the world with shared leadership responsibilities in the wider international system. "The Trilateral Commission is international ... (and) ... is intended to be the vehicle for multinational consolidation of the commercial and banking interests by seizing control of the political government of the United States." [*With No Apologies*, by Senator Barry Goldwater]

Bilderberg Group – The Bilderberg is a quasi-secret consortium of international bankers, politicians, academics and business persons who meet annually to plan world economic and political policies. The Bilderberg has no membership per se but attendees who have been invited by the steering committee sometimes year-after-year. American politicians routinely attend even through it violates the Logan Act prohibiting office holders from conducting secret meetings where policy decisions are discussed and made.

THE 'HIDDEN HAND' OF FREEMASONRY

WASHINGTON — BONAPARTE — MARX — STALIN

Freemasonry – Quasi-secret society in that exists publicly but its criminality and secrets are only revealed to higher level members. All are bound to secrecy in a blood oath and members work to advance each other in business and politics especially the courts, police and local, state and federal governments. Created the 1st "gang sign" the masonic "Hidden Hand" found in tens of dozens of portraits and photographs of prominent masons including those guilty of the murder of tens of millions through war and forced socialism/communism.

Skull & Bones – Secret society at Yale University created and endowed by opium dealers (Russell Trust) that "taps" 15 new members each junior class. Membership includes 3 US Presidents (Bush Sr., Bush Jr. and Taft). The 2004 Presidential election between Bush Jr. and John Kerry was between two members of an organization that has less than 600 living alumni at any one time.

Bohemian Club – Famous for its roster of past US Presidents, power brokers, and their Bohemian Grove retreat where members encamp in a private, secure redwood grove in California for 2 weeks (3 weekends) in July and burn a child in effigy in an occult ritual known as "Cremation of Care".

Other Organizations & Groups of Interest: Pilgrim Society & Supranational Top 400, Rhodes Scholars – Talent identification and scholarship program for Cecil Rhodes' round table groups, Dual-Citizen Zionist Israelis – Political Zionists invest in American politicians and media companies who then lobby and vote for sending billions to Israel. Talpiot Companies/CEOs and Sayanim.

Berggruen Institute - Claimed to be the new Bilderberg on their website and then took it down, Intelligence agency alumni (I.E. CIA Democrats) being funded for Congressional campaigns.

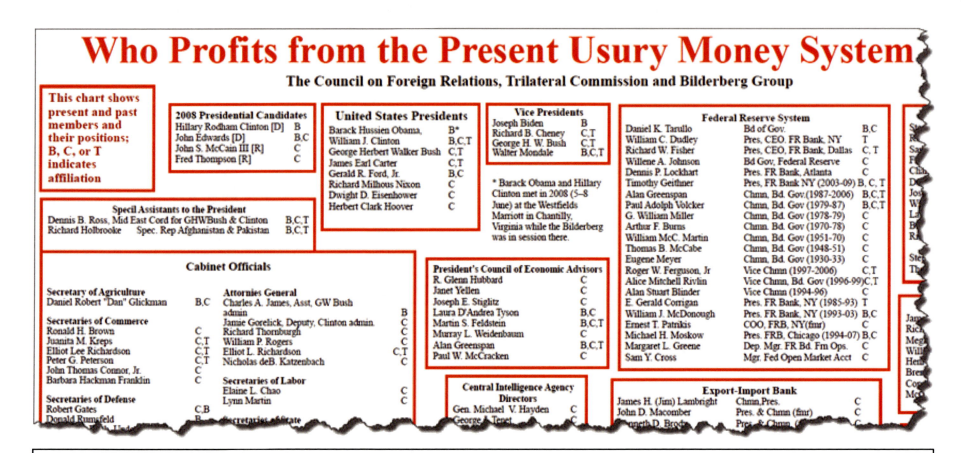

2010 Bilderberg, CFR, Trilateral Commission Membership Chart by the **Fund to Restore an Educated Electorate** – Organized crime's hidden government AKA the "Deep State". Shows multi-decade unbroken control of key power centers through both "Democrat" and "Republican" administrations. The rest of chart includes: Universities, Congress, Unions, Federal Judiciary, National Security Council, Media, The World Bank, IMF, Financial Institutions, Joint Chiefs of Staff, Religious Leaders, and 9-11 Commission, and others. Get the entire, expanded high resolution version from The Liberator:
https://www.dropbox.com/s/xx0vs2f2w40u7yl/2010%20Bilderberg%20CFR%20Trilateral%20Chart.pdf?dl=0
We are looking for a donor interested in sponsoring an updated version with free masons, Skull & Bones, dual-citizen Zionist Israelis, Berggruen Institute, and Bohemian Grove members identified as well. Serious Inquiries Only!

"Government" - The Biggest Scam in History Exposed is both a book and series of one-page visual overviews of concepts hidden from the public by inter-generational organized crime that has been controlling the flow of information in society. Their "Propaganda Matrix" includes control of the government, "public" schools, scouting, intelligence agencies, military and police training, and a weaponized media system of 6 companies running hundreds of subsidiaries to give the population the illusion of choice and diversity-of-opinion while propagandizing, deceiving, and distracting us from the reality of our tax slavery and authoritarian control. These one-pagers are designed to be printed out and shared, but with accessible PDF versions with active hypertext links. We have an 8GB Flash Drive/Dropbox called: *The Liberator* with additional evidence of government and media criminality.

"Government"-The Biggest Scam in History Exposed: Consumer Monopoly Consolidation

www.Government-Scam.com

The Drug Dealers & the Company Store – Monopoly corporations that debilitate the population with excessive sugar, aspartame, BPA/BPS, rBGH, artificial food colorings, glyphosate, fluoridated water, glutamates, refined grains, and genetically modified ingredients many scientifically designed and marketed to be physically and psychologically addictive. Most significant industrial production of consumer goods concentrated into a handful of monopoly companies financed to be a predatory force within their own industries by the money center banks and their central bank that have bought up the world with the paper tickets they create out of thin air using fractional reserve banking. Shop Local. Break the Chains. Know Your Farmer. Grow what you can. Barter. Boycott and divest from these companies.

Diet, injections, and injunctions will combine, from a very early age, to produce the sort of character and the sort of beliefs that the authorities consider desirable, and any serious criticism of the powers that be will become psychologically impossible. Even if all are miserable, all will believe themselves happy, because the government will tell them that they are so.
– Bertrand Russell, Fabian Socialist and Eugenicist writing in *The Impact of Science on Society*, 1953

Glyphosate is the active ingredient in Monsanto's Roundup herbicide. Monsanto and Dow are chemical companies that make poisons for the military (Agent Orange) who are now adding toxic additives to the US/global food supply including glyphosate, rBGH, Aspartame, and Fluoride among others while monopolizing seed companies and genetically modifying the seeds in harmful ways in what appears to be an effort to control/poison the food supply. Glyphosate can be harmful to human beings in concentrations of as little as 0.1 parts per billion (ppb).

Charts from a story by clean food activist Vani Hari (Aka the Food Babe) foodbabe.com/2016/11/15/monsanto/

Full independent laboratory report from Food Democracy Now and the Detox Project: https://s3.amazonaws.com/media.fooddemocracynow.org/images/FDN_Glyphosate_FoodTesting_Report_p2016.pdf

Glyphosate Food Testing Results: (in parts per billion – ppb)

Full laboratory reports for this food testing can be found here. A searchable database of results can be found here.

General Mills		
Cheerios	Original Cheerios	Glyphosate – 1,125.3 ppb / AMPA – 26.4
Honey Nut Cheerios	Honey Nut Cheerios	Glyphosate – 670.2 ppb / AMPA – 14.5
Wheaties	Wheaties	Glyphosate – 31.2 ppb
Trix	Trix	Glyphosate – 9.9 ppb
Annie's	Gluten Free Bunny Cookies Cocoa & Vanilla	Glyphosate – 55.13* ppb
Kellogg's		
Corn Flakes	Corn Flakes	Glyphosate – 78.9 ppb
Raisin Bran	Raisin Bran	Glyphosate – 82.9 ppb
Kashi	Organic Promise**	Glyphosate – 24.9 ppb
Special K	Special K	Glyphosate – 74.6 ppb
Frosted Flakes	Frosted Flakes	Glyphosate – 72.8 ppb
Cheez-It	Cheez-It (Original)	Glyphosate – 24.6 ppb
Cheez-It	Cheez-It (Whole Grain)	Glyphosate – 36.25* ppb
Kashi	Soft-Baked Cookies, Oatmeal Dark Chocolate	Glyphosate – 275.58* ppb
Nabisco		
Ritz	Ritz Crackers	Glyphosate – 270.24 ppb
Triscuit	Triscuit	Glyphosate – 89.68 ppb
Oreo	Oreo Original	Glyphosate – 289.47* ppb
Nabisco (continued)		
Oreo	Oreo Double Stuf Chocolate Sandwich Cookies	Glyphosate – 140.90* ppb
Oreo	Oreo Double Stuf Golden Sandwich Cookies	Glyphosate – 215.40* ppb
PepsiCo		
Stacy's	Stacy's Simply Naked Pita Chips (Frito-Lay)	Glyphosate – 812.53 ppb
Lay's	Lay's: Kettle Cooked Original	Glyphosate – 452.71* ppb
Doritos	Doritos: Cool Ranch	Glyphosate – 481.27* ppb
Fritos	Fritos (Original) (100% Whole Grain)	Glyphosate – 174.71* ppb
Campbell Soup Company		
Goldfish	Goldfish crackers original (Pepperidge Farm)	Glyphosate – 18.40 ppb
Goldfish	Goldfish crackers colors	Glyphosate – 8.02 ppb
Goldfish	Goldfish crackers Whole Grain	Glyphosate – 24.58 ppb
Little Debbie		
Little Debbie	Oatmeal Creme Pies	Glyphosate – 264.28* ppb
Lucy's		
Lucy's	Oatmeal Cookies Gluten Free	Glyphosate – 452.44* ppb
Whole Foods		
365	365 Organic Golden Round Crackers**	Glyphosate – 119.12* ppb
Back to Nature		
Back to Nature	Crispy Cheddar Crackers	Glyphosate – 327.22* ppb

Limit of Quantitation: 5 ppb

*These samples exhibit very low recovery and/or response. The above amounts found are rough estimates at best and may not represent an accurate representation of the sample.

** Widespread contamination in food supply – even organic farmers are having their crops/ our food contaminated.

In October of 2018 another 3rd party, independent test commissioned by the nonprofit Environmental Working Group found Glyphosate in 28 out of 28 samples of oat-based cereals and oat-based food marketed to children.

"Government" - The Biggest Scam in History Exposed is both a book and series of one-page visual overviews of concepts hidden from the public by inter-generational organized crime that has been controlling the flow of information in society. Their "Propaganda Matrix" includes control of the government, "public" schools, scouting, intelligence agencies, military and police training, and a weaponized media system of 6 companies running hundreds of subsidiaries to give the population the illusion of choice and diversity-of-opinion while propagandizing, deceiving, and distracting us from the reality of our tax slavery and authoritarian control. These one-pagers are designed to be printed out and shared, but with accessible PDF versions with active hypertext links. We have an 8GB Flash Drive/Dropbox called: *The Liberator* with additional evidence of government and media criminality.

"Government"-The Biggest Scam in History Exposed:
Understanding Genetically Modified Organisms (GMOs) and Monopoly Seed Consolidation
www.Government-Scam.com

Executive Summary

Control of the food supply is a well-known tactic for controlling populations. The Soviet dictator Joseph Stalin engineered a forced famine in Ukraine to crush its independence movement killing over 7 million. Many intelligent observers detect what looks like a pattern of chemical companies that make poisons for the military (Bayer/Monsanto and DowDuPont) being financed by the largest banks and foundations focused on population control putting and/or testing harmful chemicals for the food supply including:

- Aspartame – Toxic sweetener linked to Donald Rumsfeld - **Monsanto**
- rBGH – Toxic GMO growth hormone for dairy production - **Monsanto**
- Fluoride – Toxic fumigant sprayed on crops – **Dow Agri-sciences** (since divested)
- Glyphosate – Toxic herbicide linked to cancer, tumors – **Monsanto**
- GMO Seeds – Using genetics to modify seeds in ways that can be harmful to humans – **Monsanto, Bayer, DowDuPont**
- Neonicotinoids pesticides – Toxic pesticides linked to massive global die-off of bees – **Bayer & DowDuPont**
- V-GURT "Terminator Seeds" – Patented, tested & on-hold for now - **Monsanto**

Genetically Modified Organisms (GMOs) are organisms, typically plants and their seeds, that have been modified at the genetic level to be different from their organic counterparts. The modifications include withstanding the direct application of herbicide and/or to produce an insecticide. However, new technologies are now being used to artificially develop other traits in plants, such as a resistance to browning in apples, and to create new organisms using synthetic biology. Despite biotech industry promises, there is no evidence that any of the GMOs currently on the market offer increased yield, drought tolerance, enhanced nutrition, or any other consumer benefit while much evidence exists that many are harmful to human health and could be debilitating the population to sicken and dumb them down.

Monsanto – A chemical company that produced chemical warfare agents for the military notably Agent Orange which was used to unethically defoliate Vietnam and kill crops, that now controls much of the world's food supply through control of seed companies and production of the world's leading herbicide Roundup whose main ingredient Glyphosate has been linked to cancer. The company also manufactures or has manufactured other toxic food additives/herbicides/GMOs tied to human health issues including rBGH, DDT, Saccharine, Aspartame, PCBs, and others.

Bayer – German multi-national that developed chemical weapons for the German military in WWI (Chlorine Gas) and, after a merger in 1925 with other chemical companies became IG Farben which produced the chemical weapons Sarin and Zyklon B among others and operated the Auschwitz III slave labor camp in WWII. 24 Farben Directors were indicted in the Nuremberg trials and the company split up and was reconstituted into Bayer. Crimes continued into the modern age: Selling knowingly contaminated blood products, Medicaid fraud, and multiple products linked to harmful side-effects and death including the drugs Trasylol, Yaz/Yasmin birth control, and bee-killing neonicotinoid pesticides.

Dow-DuPont – Other chemical companies that have produced chemical weapons for the military (Agent Orange, Napalm B) that are involved with monopolizing the seed industry and selling GMO seeds.

9/17/12 Seralini Paper Showing rats developing massive tumors when fed glyphosate and/or GMOs published in Food And Chemical Toxicology after being reviewed by scientific peers.

early 2013 Richard E. Goodman, a former Monsanto researcher with close ties to the biotech industry, joins the senior editorial staff of FCT.

11/28/13 FCT announces it is retracting the Seralini study.

Write the journal @ bit.ly/1brYs9N and let them know we expect them to support independent peer reviewed studies and not allow their board to be controlled by corporations.

"Diet, injections, and injunctions will combine, from a very early age, to produce the sort of character and the sort of beliefs that the authorities consider desirable, and any serious criticism of the powers that be will become psychologically impossible. Even if all are miserable, all will believe themselves happy, because the government will tell them that they are so." -Bertrand Russel, The Impact of Science on Society, 1953

The Seralini Paper was a two-year study of Monsanto's Roundup ready NK603 corn and Roundup Glyphosate-based herbicide by a team lead by Giles-Eric Séralini of the University of Caen. The study was first published in the journal Food and Chemical Toxicology (F&CT) and found that rats feed the Roundup treated GMO corn developed significantly more tumors and died prematurely compared to rats in the control group. After "former" Monsanto researcher Richard Goodman joined the staff of F&CT and an "Astroturf" PR campaign of paid/influenced "third-party" experts, the journal retracted the study. The authors received offers from four other peer-reviewed journals to republish and chose Environmental Sciences Europe. The affair is both illustrative of the harmful nature of Monsanto's GMO seeds and Glyphosate-based herbicides and how moneyed organized crime interests can control perception by having damaging information concealed from the public.

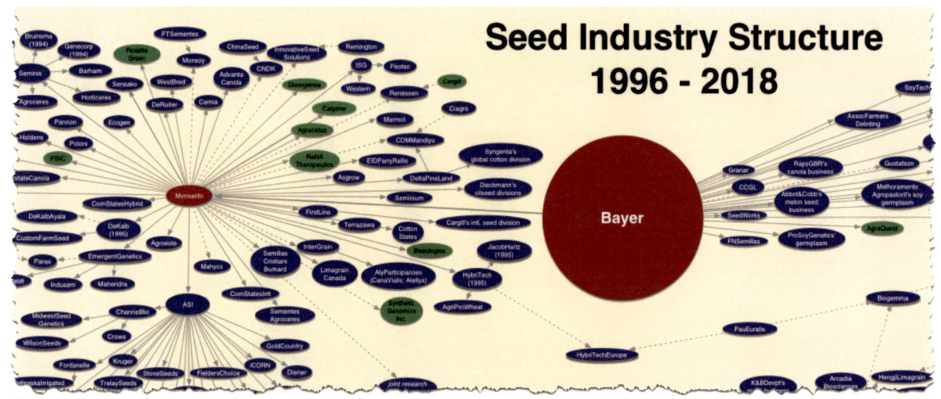

This visualization was created by Dr. Phillip Howard, a professor at MSU studying the global food system, shows monopolization of the seed industry (200+ companies acquired) by companies that have specialized in making chemical weapons (CW) for the military and neonicotinoid insecticides (NIs) linked to pollinating bee die-offs, including: **Monsanto** (CW: Agent Orange, White Phosphorus) and **Bayer** (CW: Chlorine Gas, Sarin, Zyklon-B & NIs) what appears to be a plan to control and weaponize the food supply. The rest of visualization, available Here and in *The Liberator* folder: Banking Cartel's Monopoly Consolidation, shows further monopolization by other military chemical weapons and neonicotinoid insecticide producers: **Dow** (CW: Agent Orange, Napalm-B, NIs) and **DuPont**. Note: Monsanto and Bayer have merged as have Dow and DuPont further monopolizing and consolidating these industries. Dr. Howard's other work shows monopolization of Beer, Wine, Meat Processing, Soft Drinks, Wheat & Bread, and Organic foods.

"Government" - The Biggest Scam in History Exposed is both a book and series of one-page visual overviews of concepts hidden from the public by inter-generational organized crime that has been controlling the flow of information in society. Their "Propaganda Matrix" includes control of the government, "public" schools, scouting, intelligence agencies, military and police training, and a weaponized media system of 6 companies running hundreds of subsidiaries to give the population the illusion of choice and diversity-of-opinion while propagandizing, deceiving, and distracting us from the reality of our tax slavery and authoritarian control. These one-pagers are designed to be printed out and shared, but with accessible PDF versions with active hypertext links. We have an 8GB Flash Drive/Dropbox called: *The Liberator* with additional evidence of government and media criminality.

"Government"-The Biggest Scam in History Exposed:
Anarchy and Voluntaryism – The Biggest Secret in American Politics
www.Government-Scam.com

Anarchy doesn't mean "No Rules", It literally means "No Rulers" but, because the organized crime "Rulers" don't want the public to know there is an option on the menu called "No Rulers" they have used their media and propaganda system to change the meaning of the word: "No Rulers" to mean: Chaos and Dystopia. The practice started in France where the organized crime government of 1893 passed the Lois scelerates ("villainous laws") that made it illegal to even use the word: Anarchist. Now organized crime uses their control of the media, Wikipedia, and even the dictionary to confuse the public by associating Anarchy with everything from violence to communism. The Canadian police were caught staging violence with police dressed as "anarchists" during protests against the G8 in Montebello in 2007.

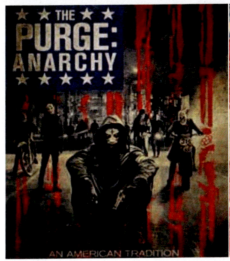

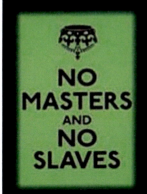

The weaponized media propaganda system would have you believe that Anarchy is something to be feared because without "Gubernare Mente"/Government there would be Mad Max chaos and murder in the streets. The reality is Anarchy is a philosophy of peace where most anarchists believe in the NonAggression Principal where initiating violence is illegitimate except in self-defense or protection of property. In a world without rulers there would still be both a market for justice and armed protective services but without monopoly government the protectors would only be focused on real crime (not victimless crimes or road piracy) and they would not delusionally believe they have rights that others don't and could be fired immediately at the first sign of abuse. Many legal theorists believe anarchy would lead to dramatically less crime and violence in society with more prosperity for all.

The word "Liberal" went through a similar weaponization. The root word is Liber which means "free" and early Liberals were similarly politically to today's small government "libertarians". Because organized crime didn't want the public to know there was an option on the menu called: "free" or "libertarian", they used their control of the media to popularize the word to mean "leftist". The word "libertarian" is, in many ways, a re-branding of the word liberal after it was weaponized and hijacked. Many older advocates of freedom refuse to part with such a noble word and refer to themselves to this day as "Classical Liberals" to denote the difference.

Voluntaryism (The "Re-Brand") – A political and social philosophy that all forms of human association should be voluntary and based on the Non-Aggression Principal (NAP) that posits that any initiation of violence on peaceful people is illegitimate, no matter what the outcome, but allows for the use of force in self-defense or to protect property. In a voluntaryist society all the "services" provided by government — from protection to roads to charity — would be better provided by voluntary interaction, the free market, and real charity.

Understanding Propaganda - The Dictionary as a Weapon

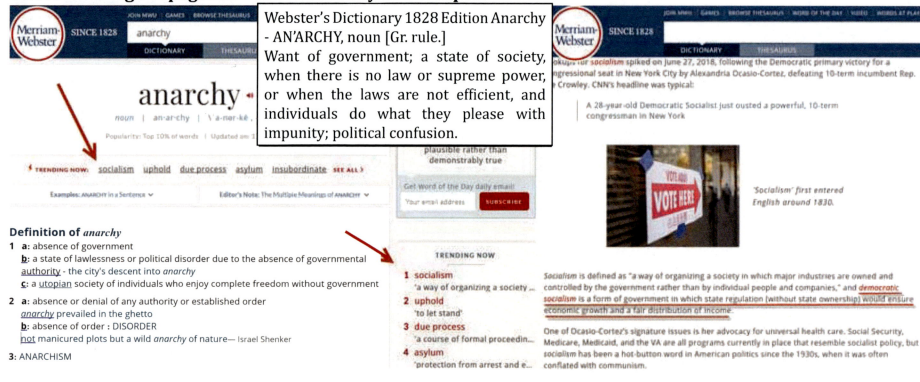

Webster's Dictionary 1828 Edition Anarchy - AN'ARCHY, noun [Gr. rule.]
Want of government; a state of society, when there is no law or supreme power, or when the laws are not efficient, and individuals do what they please with impunity; political confusion.

"The basic tool for the manipulation of reality is the manipulation of words. If you can control the meaning of words, you can control the people who must use the words." - Philip K. Dick

The Merriam-Webster Dictionary is owned by Encyclopedia Britannica which is owned by the Safra banking family where Leslie Gelb, President Emeritus of the Council on Foreign Relations sits on the Editorial Board of Advisors. You can understand the weaponization of language by comparing the 1828 Webster's Dictionary definition of Anarchy with the current definition from Merriam-Webster's on-line dictionary which has been promoting a pro-Statist version of the word: Socialism in the "Trending Now" section, the #1 spot available to promote a specific word/concept, for over a month as of this writing. Their own definition of "democratic socialism" laughably claims **"would ensure economic growth and a fair distribution of income"**. Technically any kind of socialism only achieves "redistribution", at the point of a gun, and "fair" to whom? Who decides? The Bankers and CFR members who own/control Merriam-Webster? Their definition of Socialism also falsely claims that "socialism" was "conflated" with communism when communism IS, by definition, socialism. Compare their claim of socialist "fairness" to their misrepresentation of Anarchy as "Utopian" and something that "prevailed in the ghetto."

"Government" - The Biggest Scam in History Exposed is both a book and series of one-page visual overviews of concepts hidden from the public by inter-generational organized crime that has been controlling the flow of information in society. Their "Propaganda Matrix" includes control of the government, "public" schools, scouting, intelligence agencies, military and police training, and a weaponized media system of 6 companies running hundreds of subsidiaries to give the population the illusion of choice and diversity-of-opinion while propagandizing, deceiving, and distracting us from the reality of our tax slavery and authoritarian control. These one-pagers are designed to be printed out and shared but with accessible PDF versions with active hypertext links. We have an 8GB Flash Drive/Dropbox called: The Liberator with additional evidence of government and media criminality.

"Government"-The Biggest Scam in History Exposed: False Flag Terrorism for War and Domestic Police State

www.Government-Scam.com

Executive Summary

The organized crime government through the FBI, intelligence agencies, and in partnership with the media, is constantly menacing the population with both real false flag terrorism where people are killed and property destroyed (9-11, Oklahoma City Bombing, 1993 World Trade Center Bombing,) and hoax events (Boston Marathon Bombing, Sandy Hook, Orlando Pulse Nightclub) where government agencies and the media present large-scale mass casualty exercises skillfully edited and presented as real events with crisis actors and invented victims.

False flag terror, hoax terror, and engineered wars are used to menace the population so they rally around the government for "security" while using the events to bring in even more police state measures which allow organized crime to tighten their control over society for the day when the game is exposed or economic conditions get so bad the population rebels.

These false flag events and hoaxes are being exposed by independent researchers who are sharing evidence and analysis over the internet. In 2018 these independent researchers began to see massive censorship and complete take downs of their YouTube channels, Facebook profiles, pages, and groups, twitter bans, and search engine and social media shenanigans. Many of the best documentaries and video evidence of government criminality have been deleted off YouTube, Vimeo, Facebook and other platforms.

We have organized two Dropboxes that can be downloaded to Flash drives or 8GB DVDs with evidence of government criminality. Please make a copy ASAP.

Fake Mass Shootings for Gun Control: Sandy Hook – Newtown, CT - Dec 14th, 2012, Orlando Pulse Nightclub – June 12th 2016, Borderline Bar and Grill - Nov 8th 2018, Las Vegas Route 91 Mass Shooting - Oct. 1st, 2017, Parkland, FL (Stoneman-Douglas HS) – Feb 14th, 2018, San Bernadino, CA – Dec 2nd 2015

False Flag Terrorism for War and Domestic Police State: September 11th, 2001 False Flag, Boston Marathon Bombing - April 15th, 2013, Oklahoma City Bombing - April 19th, 1995, 1993 World Trade Center Car Bomb -Feb 26th, 1993, ISIS, AlQaeda, and Syrian Fake Gas Attacks

If you don't understand that the MainStreamMedia, Google and major Internet social media platforms are tools of organized crime and deceiving you soviet-style then you aren't even in the game. There is no other option but to research these events for yourself. In the internet age, ignorance is a choice!

Key Concepts

1. Control of perception is the most powerful weapon in organized crime's arsenal. Can the tell-lie-vision & glossy magazines make you believe the system is legitimate, that you are not a free human being but an "American", that you "owe taxes", that the elections aren't rigged, that you are physically in danger from "terrorists" to get you to support police state measures, that mass shootings are rampant so peaceful people must turn in their guns, etc.

2. The CIA's program to control the media that was exposed in the 1976 Church Committee hearings was rumored to be called, and has become widely referred to, as: Operation Mockingbird. The speculation is that if organized crime can control the "head ends" of the information food chain (the biggest wire services, "news" networks, "newspapers of record", etc.) then all the regional television stations, radio station, and local newspapers will simply "mockingbird" what the bigger media outlets report. Concurrently, most people (who don't understand the "big con") will simply "mockingbird" what the MainStreamMedia and internet publications say.

3. We break down how organized crime has monopolized ownership of the media into six different companies running hundreds of subsidiaries in The Propaganda Matrix. We break down how organized crime controls editorial content in Control of the Media. We include the article How the CIA Made Google in: The Liberator

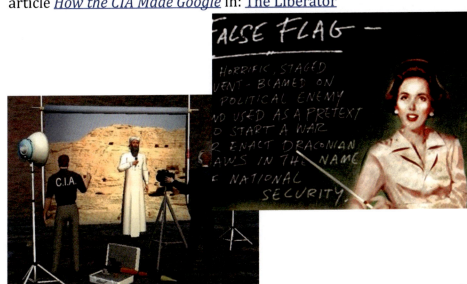

Hoax Event - Boston Marathon Bombing

Left: James "Bim" Costello, **Middle**: Kyle Larrow, **Right**: Close up of Nicole Brannock Gross's shirt. All displaying impossible prop clothing where allegedly pipe bomb shrapnel/blast shredded the fabric of the clothing but did no damage to the skin underneath. Costello's shirt shows impossible clean vertical cuts.

What Really Happened: Gov't mass casualty exercise using special effects & traitorous amputee crisis actors, FBI agents/police that was photographed/edited by select news agencies and then sold to the population as a real event.

Used to Justify: Police state measures: Roll-out of pre-purchased armored vehicles for American cities and towns, beta-test of searching homes without warrants and locking down an American city with Hollywood trickery.

Best Evidence of Fakery: Thorndike photos expose no real injuries in aftermath, Bauman's legs not bleeding after explosion, no more than 3-4 dozen crisis actors photographed around "blast" sites vs official total of 264 injured, plainclothes but identified FBI agents keeping uninvolved police/people away.

Best Documentary: *The Boston Marathon Unbombing* by PlasmaBurns
Best Short Videos: PlasmaBurns series exposing major crisis actor "Heroes" and "Victims" including: Baumann, Downes, Corcorans, Gregory, Valverdes, FBI Caught Redhanded at Boston Bombing, Reporting the FBI to the FBI.
Best Books: *And Nobody Died in Boston*, Either (Fetzer)

False Flag Event – September 11th, 2001

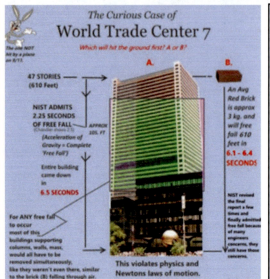

WTC7 was a modern, fireproofed steel-frame building not struck by a plane that collapsed completely, and symmetrically into its own footprint at 5:20 PM. The building fell at free-fall speed defying the laws of physics and displaying all the hallmarks of a controlled demolition: Visible squibs, free-fall collapse, molten metal. At 5:00 Fox News, CNN and the BBC began reporting it had already fell. Whistleblower Barry Jennings reported bombs. Prior knowledge, auditory explosions, symmetrical collapse.

What Really Happened: Both towers and WTC 7 brought down in controlled demolitions organized by US & Israeli intelligence agencies with media cover up.

Used to Justify: Wars in Afghanistan and Iraq, warrantless wiretapping, suspension of posse comitatus and habeas corpus, torture, military tribunals.

Best Evidence of Gov't involvement: Obvious use of explosives in buildings: free fall speeds, molten metal still molten weeks later, explosive residue in dust, dozens of war games taking place on 9-11 to pull fighter response/distract FAA, Israeli Mossad (Aka Dancing Israelis) caught "documenting the event", symmetrical collapse.

Best Documentaries: *Anatomy of a Great Deception*, *AE911Truth: Experts Speak Out*, *Solving 9-11* by Chris Bollyn

Best Short Videos: *9-11: A Conspiracy Theory*, *9-11 Trillions - Follow the $*

Books: 9-11 Ten Years Later (DRG), Another 19 (Ryan), Solving 9-11(Bollyn)

"Government" - The Biggest Scam in History Exposed is both a book and series of one-page visual overviews of concepts hidden from the public by inter-generational organized crime that has been controlling the flow of information in society. Their "Propaganda Matrix" includes control of the government, "public" schools, scouting, intelligence agencies, military and police training, and a weaponized media system of 6 companies running hundreds of subsidiaries and Google/YouTube/Fedbook and others to give the population the illusion of diversity of opinion while propagandizing, deceiving, and distracting us from the reality of our tax slavery and authoritarian control. These one-pagers are designed to be printed out and shared but with accessible PDF versions with active hypertext links. We have an 8GB Flash Drive/Dropbox called: *The Liberator* with additional evidence of government and media criminality.

"Government"-The Biggest Scam in History Exposed: The Basics for Police, Judges, and Government Employees

www.Government-Scam.com

A one-page "clip & copy" overview for police, judges, and government employees that explains the basics of government criminality. PDF version with links to the evidence available for free on our website.

Dear Police, Judges, and Government Employees,
Our sincerest apologies for having to be the ones to explain this but you have been tricked into supporting a system set up by inter-generational organized crime to rob you, your family, friends, and neighbors. "Government" isn't something that was set up to help or protect society. "Government is a system that has been used for thousands of years to rob and control society. The root words from Latin are:
Gubernare = "To Control" & Mente = "The Mind" = Mind Control
Organized crime's mind control program starts with controlling the information you have received since birth through control of education and a weaponized monopoly media and propaganda system. The government's mandatory "public schools" and accredited private/parochial schools use an educational model developed in 19th century Prussia (now Germany) to indoctrinate a pseudo-religion, Statism, and obedience to an organized crime system that called itself monarchy. When the scam of monarchy /"divine right of kings" was exposed, organized crime developed "democracy" to trick the people into thinking they are in charge but easily controlling the outcome of elections through control of the media, disparity of campaign funds, blackmail, bribery, assassination, and other means. Democracy itself is an illegitimate concept because nothing, not even if the majority believe it to be so, can make something inherently immoral (theft, extortion, caging non-violent individual for victimless crimes, etc.) "moral" just because the majority of people decide to vote for something in a political ritual. Just because the mob wants to lynch black folks or rob Peter to pay Paul doesn't make those obvious crimes moral just because the perpetrators outnumber their victims.
The "Gubernare Mente" program raised you to believe that it is OK for you to use violence, extortion and taxation (theft) on overwhelmingly peaceful people because some people are tricked into voting for "government". You have been conned, duped and "chumped" into participating in an obviously immoral system and robbing your friends and neighbors.
What Should You Do? 1. Immediately stop enforcement of victimless crimes and road piracy. 2. Find another job 3. Sabotage any system that lets organized crime rob, tax, track, trace or control peaceful people.

The Basics of "Gubernare Mente", Voting and Morality

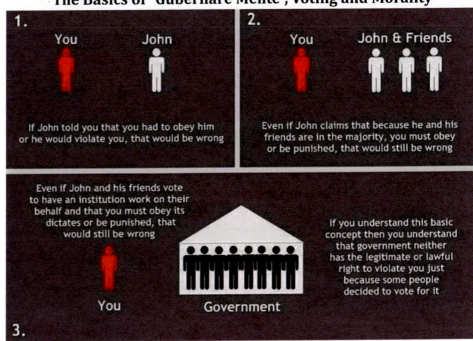

1. If you don't have the moral right to make up rules for everyone (laws) or boss people around or steal their money then you can't delegate rights that you don't have yourself to a "representative" or a "government".
2. If it is impossible for "We the People" to have delegated the ability to rob and control people to government then where did "government' get rights that the people don't have themselves? Hint: They don't!, they're criminals and, mostly, unwitting/willfully ignorant victims of "Gubernare Mente".
3. The idea that people must pay your salaries, taxes, fines, pensions and obey your laws (politician scribbles) because hundreds of years ago a couple of dozen slave owners on a continent of three million people got together in a room and wrote down on a fancy piece of paper that they alone get to make up rules for everyone and steal the wealth of others is ridiculous on its face. No one signed any "social contract". It's been a scam from the beginning.
4. Organized crime has been reinforcing this belief system through six monopoly media companies running hundreds of subsidiaries to give you the illusion of choice / diversity-of-information. Click Here for Evidence.
5. Organized crime controls the content of propaganda through organizations including the CIA, CFR, and Bilderberg Group. Click Here for Evidence.

The Basics In Memes

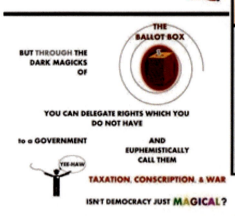

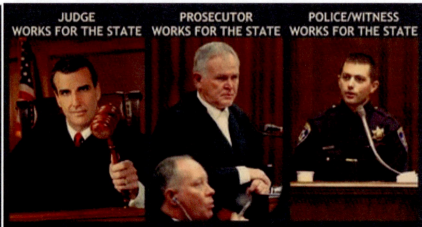

The Good News Alternative: Voluntaryism! - The world is a self-organizing system that produces spontaneous order and that all the "services" provided by government - from protection to roads to charity - can be better provided by voluntary interaction, the free market, and real charity.

"Government" - The Biggest Scam in History Exposed is both a book and series of one-page visual overviews of concepts hidden from the public by inter-generational organized crime that has been controlling the flow of information in society. Their "Propaganda Matrix" includes control of the government, "public" schools, scouting, intelligence agencies, military and police training, and a weaponized media system of 6 companies running hundreds of subsidiaries to give the population the illusion of choice and diversity-of-opinion while propagandizing, deceiving, and distracting us from the reality of our tax slavery and authoritarian control. These one-pagers are designed to be printed out and shared, but with accessible PDF versions with active hypertext links. We have an 8GB Flash Drive/Dropbox called: The Liberator with additional evidence of government and media criminality.

Ross Ulbricht

Ross Ulbricht, a peaceful 32-year-old entrepreneur was given a sentence of double life without parole for the non-violent, victimless crime of running a website that matched willing buyers and willing sellers outside of government/organized crime's purview. No victims could be named at trial. Silk Road was a web commerce platform based on the voluntaryist philosophy of free markets, where people the world over could trade bitcoin for a variety of goods, not all of them legal in every jurisdiction.

https://freeross.org/

Peter Steinmetz & Thomas "Morpheus" Constanzo

Phoenix-area neurologist Peter Steinmetz (left) and bitcoin entrepreneur Thomas "Morpheus" Constanzo (right) arrested with operating an "unlicensed bitcoin exchange" I.E. for selling bitcoins, strings of letters and numbers, for cash to willing buyers. Another completely victimless crime where the State entraps someone and claims their peaceful economic exchange is illegal to benefit a private central bank that lobbied and bribed Congress for a monopoly privilege that steals from everyone else.

https://www.titanians.org/my-friend-morpheus/
Donate to Thomas "Morpheus" Constanzo
Via PayPal: borisheir@yahoo.com
Via Bitcoin: 1CnMqpF3dUoHSUg3r4ngAsJoNhSTBU7TY

Michael Edwards

Michael Edwards is a father, a brother, a son; a good man. He is loved and supported by family and friends and has been locked behind bars for 24 years of a 60 year sentence for selling $850 of cocaine back in the 90's to a disgruntled girlfriend.

https://www.change.org/p/rick-scott-give-michael-edwards-his-life-back

Call/ Write and Request Clemency:
Gov. Rick Scott
400 S Monroe St,
Tallahassee, FL 32399
Phone:(850) 717-9337

Whistleblowers, Confessions, and Quotes
"Surely if there was a conspiracy this vast then someone would have talked"

American history is replete with whistleblowers who have courageously risked their lives to bring organized crime's activities to the public's attention but whose testimony has been buried by the "propaganda matrix" of the controlled "news" and 24 x7 distractions of weaponized media and children's games played by adults. Here are some quotes from those who have tried to warn us or confessions from the criminals themselves.

"Since I entered politics, I have chiefly had men's views confided to me privately. Some of the biggest men in the United States, in the field of commerce and manufacture, are afraid of something. They know that there is a power somewhere so organized, so subtle, so watchful, so interlocked, so complete, so pervasive, that they better not speak above their breath when they speak in condemnation of it."

Woodrow Wilson,
Former President of the United States
The New Freedom

"For more than a century, ideological extremists at either end of the political spectrum have seized upon well-publicized incidents such as my encounter with Castro to attack the Rockefeller family for the inordinate influence they claim we wield over American political and economic institutions. Some even believe we are part of a secret cabal working against the best interests of the United States, characterizing my family and me as internationalists and of conspiring with others around the world to build a more integrated global political and economic structure - one world, if you will. If that is the charge, I stand guilty, and I am proud of it."
- **David Rockefeller**, banker and oil monopolist
- Memoirs, 2003, Page 406

"The real menace of our Republic is the invisible government, which like a giant octopus sprawls its slimy legs over our cities, states and nation. To depart from mere generalizations, let me say that at the head of this octopus are the Rockefeller–Standard Oil interests and a small group of powerful banking houses generally referred to as the international bankers. The little coterie of powerful international bankers virtually run the United States government for their own selfish purposes. They practically control both parties, write political platforms, make catspaws of party leaders, use the leading men of private organizations, and resort to every device to place in nomination for high public office only such candidates as will be amenable to the dictates of corrupt big business. These international bankers and Rockefeller–Standard Oil interests control the majority of the newspapers and magazines in this country. They use the columns of these papers to club into submission or drive out of office public officials who refuse to do the bidding of the powerful corrupt cliques which compose the invisible government. It operates under cover of a self-created screen [and] seizes our executive officers, legislative bodies, schools, courts, newspapers and every agency created for the public protection.
- **John F. Hylan**, New York City Mayor
- Speech transcribed in *New York Times* article:
Hylan adds Pinchot to Presidency List, Foresees a Revolt, Dec 10th 1922

Edward Bernays,
Pioneer of Corporate PR and Propaganda

"Those who manipulate this unseen mechanism of society constitute an invisible government which is the true ruling power of our country. ...We are governed, our minds are molded, our tastes formed, our ideas suggested, largely by men we have never heard of. This is a logical result of the way in which our democratic society is organized. Vast numbers of human beings must cooperate in this manner if they are to live together as a smoothly functioning society. ...In almost every act of our daily lives, whether in the sphere of politics or business, in our social conduct or our ethical thinking, we are dominated by the relatively small number of persons...who understand the mental processes and social patterns of the masses. It is they who pull the wires which control the public mind."

"The governments of the present day have to deal not merely with other governments, with emperors, kings and ministers, but also with the secret societies which have everywhere their unscrupulous agents, and can at the last moment upset all the governments' plans. "
- **British Prime Minister Benjamin Disraeli**, 1876 - Wikiquote

"Behind the ostensible government sits enthroned an Invisible government owing no allegiance and acknowledging no responsibility to the people. To destroy this invisible government, to befoul this unholy alliance between corrupt business and corrupt politics is the first task of the statesmanship of today."
– **Theodore Roosevelt**, US President
The Progressive Covenant with the People speech, 1912- Audio – Library of Congress

"In March, 1915, the J.P. Morgan interests, the steel, shipbuilding, and powder interest, and their subsidiary organizations, got together 12 men high up in the newspaper world and employed them to select the most influential newspapers in the United States and sufficient number of them to control generally the policy of the daily press.... They found it was only necessary to purchase the control of 25 of the greatest papers. "An agreement was reached; the policy of the papers was bought, to be paid for by the month; an editor was furnished for each paper to properly supervise and edit information regarding the questions of preparedness, militarism, financial policies, and other things of national and international nature considered vital to the interests of the purchasers."
- **Oscar Callaway**, U.S. Congressman
Congressional Record of February 9, 1917, page 2947

"The real truth of the matter is, as you and I know, that a financial element in the larger centers has owned the Government ever since the days of Andrew Jackson."
– **Franklin Delano Roosevelt,** US President
Letter to Col. Edward Mandell House (21 November 1933);
as quoted in F.D.R.: His Personal Letters, 1928-1945,
edited by Elliott Roosevelt (New York: Duell, Sloan and Pearce, 1950), pg. 373.

" From the days of Spartacus-Weishaupt to those of Karl Marx, and down to Trotsky (Russia), Bela Kun (Hungary), Rosa Luxembourg (Germany), and Emma Goldman (United States), this world-wide conspiracy for the overthrow of civilisation and for the reconstitution of society on the basis of arrested development, of envious malevolence, and impossible equality, has been steadily growing. It played, as a modern writer, Mrs. Webster, has so ably shown, a definitely recognisable part in the tragedy of the French Revolution. It has been the mainspring of every subversive movement during the Nineteenth Century; and now at last this band of extraordinary personalities from the underworld of the great cities of Europe and America have gripped the Russian people by the hair of their heads and have become practically the undisputed masters of that enormous empire."
-**Winston Churchill**, Prime Minster UK
Zionism vs. Bolshevism, Illustrated Sunday Herald, February 8th 1920, Page 5

Meme War

Here is some intellectual ammo that you can screenshot and post to social media or share selectively with friends and family. Sometimes a picture... or a meme is worth 1000 words.

Check out the folder: "Dank Liberty Memes" on our Dropbox / Flash Drive of Freedom: *The Liberator*

The Basics – To help others understand Voluntaryist principles and thought. Here are the basics. If your government teacher or professor challenges the logic, morality and principals then ask them publicly: "The Five Questions", political philosopher Larken Rose's challenge to ethics, civics and government professors and teachers who support the state.

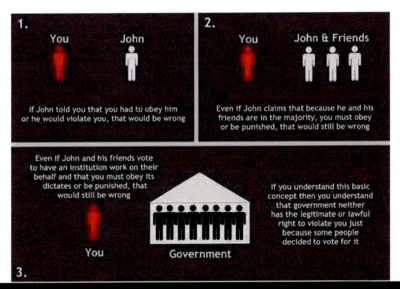

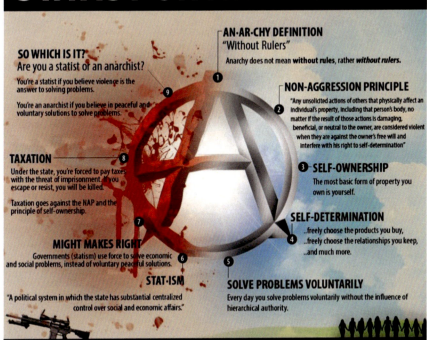

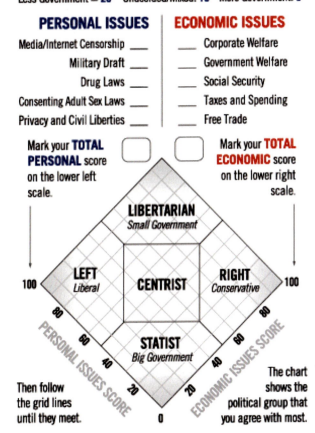

The weaponized media system and their fake news broadcasts would lead you to believe that the political spectrum is either left or right. This allows them to offer you a fake "Hobson's Choice" every four year of two candidates they both own. The reality is that the political spectrum is better represented by the diamond-shaped "Nolan Chart" developed by MIT student David Nolan and popularized by the Advocates for Self-Government. You can take the quiz on their website to see where you really might land.

NATURAL LAW

Based in reality, conforms to the natural world, nature

An absolute aspect of nature, obvious as a self-evident truth

THE FIVE BASIC BREACHES OF NATURAL LAW

ASSAULT - RAPE - THEFT - TRESPASS - COERCION

All 5 transgressions constitute a theft of some sort - theft of physical well being, theft of sexual choice, theft of physical property, theft of security, theft of consent

A RIGHT

An action that causes no harm or violation of another, your rights are an attribute that constitute your property

A WRONG

An action that violates another, the theft of the rights or property of another

A RIGHT AND A WRONG ARE MUTUALLY EXCLUSIVE

Natural Law cannot be changed or subverted by the will of any being. The whim of "Legislators" only creates rules of a membership club (a society). Without a victim there is no crime. No violation, no harm, no theft of rights, equals no crime.

www.Government-Scam.com

THE FIVE QUESTIONS

Larken Rose's challenge to teachers and professors that support government

1) Is there any means by which any number of individuals can delegate to someone else the moral right to do something which none of the individuals have the moral right to do themselves?

2) Do those who wield political power (presidents, legislators, etc.) have the moral right to do things which other people do not have the moral right to do? If so, from whom and how did they acquire such a right?

3) Is there any process (e.g., constitutions, elections, legislation) by which human beings can transform an immoral act into a moral act (without changing the act itself)?

4) When law-makers and law-enforcers use coercion and force in the name of law and government, do they bear the same responsibility for their actions that anyone else would who did the same thing on his own?

5) When there is a conflict between an individual's own moral conscience, and the commands of a political authority, is the individual morally obligated to do what he personally views as wrong in order to "obey the law"?

www.Government-Scam.com

The Ridiculousness, Illogic, and Immorality of "Government" and "Democracy"

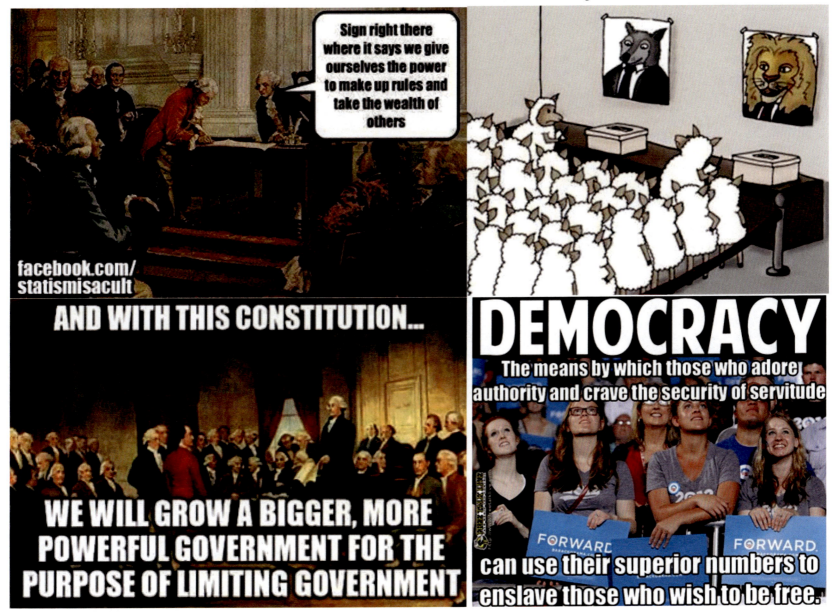

The Ridiculousness of Mandatory Government Schools

EDUCATION: Planned Enslavement Through Lack of Knowledge

"The aim of public education is not to spread enlightenment at all, it is simply to reduce as many individuals as possible to the same safe level, to breed and train a standardized citizenry, to put down dissent and originality." — H. L. Mencken 1880-1956

"I don't want a nation of thinkers. I want a nation of workers." — John D. Rockefeller
Created the General Education Board (GEB) in 1903 to dispense Rockefeller funds to education

"Silent Weapons for Quiet Wars"
EXCERPT FROM Page 7
"The quality of education given to the lower class must be of the poorest sort, so that the moat of ignorance isolating the inferior class from the superior class is and remains incomprehensible to the inferior class. With such an initial handicap, even bright lower class individuals have little if any hope of extricating themselves from their assigned lot in life. This form of slavery is essential to maintain some measure of social order, peace, and tranquillity for the ruling upper class."

Read "Silent Weapons for Quiet Wars"
www.StopTheCrime.net/source.html

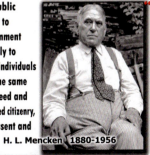

Public school is where the catechism is taught.

The Fear-Based Religion of Compulsory Public School

Church	Priests	Scriptures
Rituals	Penance	
Worship	Sacraments	God

The Honest Teacher

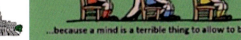

INDOCTRINATION

...because a mind is a terrible thing to allow to be free from the State.

SCHOOL
- Authoritarian structure
- Dress code
- Emphasis on silence and order
- Negative reinforcement
- Walk in lines
- Loss of individual autonomy
- Abridged freedoms
- No input in decision making
- Set times enforced for walking, eating, etc.

PRISON
- Authoritarian structure
- Dress code
- Emphasis on silence and order
- Negative reinforcement
- Walk in lines
- Loss of individual autonomy
- Abridged freedoms
- No input in decision making
- Set times enforced for walking, eating, etc.

School vs. Prison

The Ridiculousness of Not Understanding that Both Parties are Owned and Controlled by the Same Interests

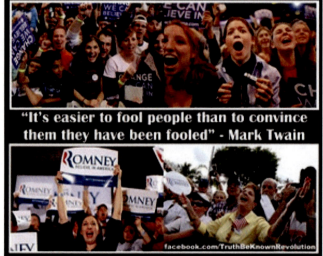

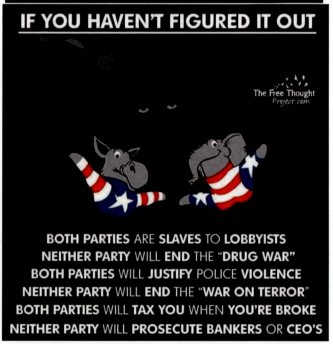

Meet the New Boss...

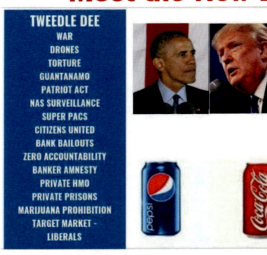

...Same as the Old Boss!

THE ONLY REAL DIFFERENCE

IS THE MARKETING STRATEGY

Make your vote for President really count! Do not choose either of the above.

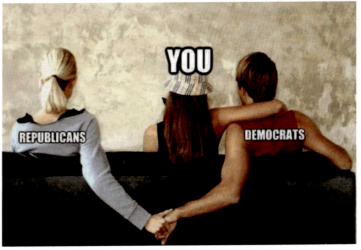

No difference between the two parties. Never forget.

The Ridiculousness of Not Understanding that the Organized Crime "Government" and the Banks, their Media Puppets and Monopoly Corporations that profit from Fractional Reserve Banking, Government-granted Monopolies, No-bid Contracts, *Mandatory* Mercury and Aluminum-Laced Vaccines, War-for-Oil, and Unnecessary "Defense" Spending Are Working Together to Loot the Tax-Slaves

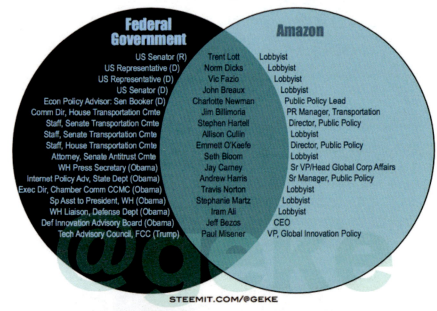

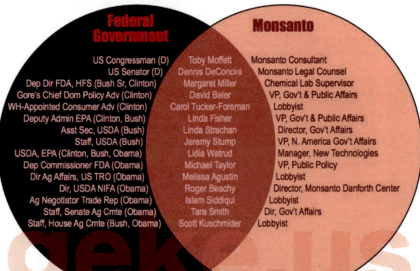

Federal Government / Big Oil

Federal Government	Name	Big Oil
Dept. of Energy (Carter)	Andrew Zausner	Dir, Government Relations (Pennzoil)
Staff: US Rep Landrieu (D)	Kevin Avery	Dir, Federal Gov't Affairs (Marathon)
Staff: US Rep Landrieu (D)	Jason Schendle	Washington Rep (API)
Staff: Sen Rockefeller (D) & Biden (D)	William Ichord	VP, Int'l Gov't Affairs (ConocoPhillips)
Staff: Sen Durbin (D) & Biden (D)	James E. Williams	Products Issues Manager (API)
Staff: Sen Lieberman (D)	Matt Gobush	Comm. Manager (ExxonMobil)
Staff: Sen Johnson (D)	Mark Rubin	Upstream Gen. Manager (API)
Staff: Rep Kilpatrick (D) & Boren (D)	Wendy Kirchoff	Dir, Fed Resources (IPAA)
Staff: Sen Feinstein (D)	Rachel Miller	Dir of Federal Affairs (BP America)
Staff: Rep DLipinski (D) & BLipinski (D)	Emily Olson	Lobbyist (BP America)
Dep Staff Dir, HGRC (Clinton)	Judith Blanchard	Fed Gov't Relations (Chevron)
Dir, House Ways & Means (Clinton)	Donna Steele Flynn	Tax Counsel (IPAA)
Dir, SEPWC (Clinton)	Lee Fuller	VP, Gov't Relations (IPAA)
Staff Economist SENRC (Clinton)	Shirley Neff	Economist (Shell Oil)
DA Sec, Dept. of Energy (Clinton)	Theresa Fariello	VP, Gov't Relations (ExxonMobil)
US: Energy for Science, DOE (Obama)	Steven Koonin	Chief Scientist (British Petroleum)

Federal Government / JP Morgan Chase

Federal Government	Name	JP Morgan Chase
US Representative (R)	Rick Lazio	Exec VP, Gov't Relations
US Senator (R)	Mel Martinez	Regional Chairman
Staff Dir, Senate Banking Cmte	Steven Patterson	VP, Gov't Relations
Sr Staff, House Financial Svs Cmte	Brendan Reilly	Managing Dir, Gov't Relations
Staff, Senate Banking Cmte	Nate Gatten	Sr VP, Gov't Relations
Sr Policy Adviser, Senate Banking Cmte	Julie Chon	Financial Analyst
SubCm Staff Dir, Senate Banking Cmte	Katherine Childress	Lobbyist
Asst US Trade Representative (Clinton)	Emily Beizer	Managing Director
Dep Asst Sec, Treasury Dept (Clinton)	Victoria Rostow	Co-Head, Fed Gov't Relations
Chief of Staff, Commerce Dept (Clinton)	Peter Scher	Exec VP & Head, Corp Responsibility
Chief of Staff, Council Econ Adv (Bush)	Pierce Scranton	Exec Dir, Gov't Relations
Asst Sec, Commerce Dept (Bush)	Nat Wienecke	VP, Gov't Relations
Dir PA, Commerce Dept (Bush)	Ann Marie Hauser	VP, Media Relations
Dep Asst Sec, Treasury Dept (Bush)	Jack Bartling	Lobbyist
Chief Information Officer, FBI (Obama)	Chad Fulgham	Info Technology Manager

Federal Government / Boeing

Federal Government	Name	Boeing
US Representative (D)	Jim Moran	Lobbyist
US Representative (R)	Todd Tiahrt	Proposal Manager
US Representative (R)	David Young	Director, Federal Legislative Affairs
US Representative (D)	Jerry Costello	Lobbyist
US Representative (D)	Norm Dicks	Lobbyist
Staff Director, House Armed Services Cmte	Bob Simmons	VP, Gov't Operations
Staff, House Armed Services Cmte	John Mulligan	Lobbyist
Staff Director, House Approp Defense Subcmte	John Shank	VP, Fed Legislative Affairs
Chief Counsel, House Energy / Commerce Cmte	Charles Ingebretson	VP, Energy Policy
Staff Director, Senate Approp Military Subcmte	Tammy Cameron	Sr VP, Gov't Relations
Staff, Senate Armed Services Cmte	Jonathan Etherton	Lobbyist
Staff, Senate Armed Services Cmte	Daniel Cox	Sr Director, Strategy
Staff, Senate Armed Services Cmte	Ryan Thompson	Lobbyist
Assoc Administrator of Regulation, FAA (Clinton)	Thomas McSweeny	Director, Int'l Regulatory Affairs
Legislative Congressional Affairs, WH (Clinton)	Timothy Keating	Exec VP, Gov't Operations
Bureau Political-Military Affairs, State Dept (Clinton)	Jeff Markey	Lobbyist
Deputy Secretary of Defense (Clinton)	Rudy de Leon	Sr VP, Gov't Affairs
Asst Administrator, FAA (Clinton)	David Traynham	Director, Commercial Regulatory Affairs
Spokesman, National Security Council (Bush)	Gordon Johndroe	VP, Gov't Operations Communications
Director Strategic Comm, State Dept (Bush)		
Assistant Secretary of State (Bush)	Sean McCormack	VP, Communications
Spokesman, National Security Council (Bush)		
Asst Secretary, Veterans Affairs Dept (Bush)	Maureen Cragin	VP, Communications
Brigadier General, Dept of Army (Bush)	Leo Brooks, Jr	VP, National Security & Space
Asst Secretary of Defense (Bush)	Mira Ricardel	VP, Strategic Missile Defense Systems
Deputy Asst Secretary of Defense (Bush)	Marlin "Buzz" Hefti	Manager, Congressional Affairs
Conduct Standards Director, Defense Dept (Bush)	Stephen Epstein	Chief Counsel, Ethics / Compliance
Sp Legislative Asst, Joint Chiefs of Staff (Bush)	Douglas Denneny	Business Development Manager
Policy Chief, Liaison Office Dept of Army (Bush)	Paul "Ted" Anderson	Lobbyist
Dep Gen Counsel, Transportation Dept (Obama)	Jennifer McIntyre	Chief Counsel, Washington Operations
Budget Liaison, Dept of Army (Obama)	John Leggieri	Lobbyist
National Security Advisor (Obama)	Gen James Jones	Board Member
Asst Secretary, Dept of Army (Obama)	Thomas Lamont	Lobbyist
Sp Asst to President on Energy, NEC (Trump)	Mike Catanzaro	Lobbyist
Deputy Secretary of Defense (Trump)	Pat Shanahan	Sr VP, Operations

Federal Government / News Media

Federal Government	Name	News Media
Public Affairs Specialist, FBI (Bush)	Brian Hale	"ABC News" Field Producer (ABC)
Press Officer, Homeland Security Dept (Bush)	Jennifer Myers	Political Unit Member (CNN)
Asst Secretary, State Dept (Bush)	Alex Feldman	VP, Affiliate Sales (CNBC)
Undersecretary of State (Bush)	Paula Dobriansky	Sr VP (Thomson Reuters)
Communications Director, WH (Bush)	Kevin Sullivan	VP, Communications (NBC Sports)
Sr Comm Advisor, Treasury Dept (Obama)	Eric Dash	Staff Reporter (New York Times)
Dep Asst to President, WH (Obama)	Kimberley Harris	Exec VP (NBC Universal Media)
Media Specialist, FEMA (Obama)	Melissa Castro	Sr Director Communications (NBC)
Asst Communications Administrator, FAA (Obama)	Sasha Johnson	Sr Political Producer (CNN)
Pentagon Press Sec, Defense Dept (Obama)	Geoff Morrell	White House Correspondent (ABC)
Comm Director, Transportation Dept (Obama)	Lynda Tran	"CBS News" Political Contributor (CBS)
Asst Secretary of Education (Obama)	Massie Ritsch	Staff Writer (Los Angeles Times)
Public Engagement Dir, Labor Dept (Obama)	Ofelia Casillas	Staff Writer (Chicago Tribune)
Comm Dir, WH Health Reform (Obama)	Linda Douglass	"ABC News" Correspondent (ABC)
Dep Asst Secretary, State Dept (Obama)	Eileen O'Connor	Moscow Bureau Chief (CNN)
Undersecretary of State (Obama)	Richard Stengel	Managing Editor (Time)
Sr Advisor to Secretary, State Dept (Obama)	Glen Johnson	Politics Editor (Boston Globe)
Asst Secretary of State (Obama)	Douglas Frantz	Investigative Reporter (New York Times)
Assistant to President, WH (Obama)	David Plouffe	"ABC News" Contributor (ABC)
WH Press Secretary (Obama)	Jay Carney	Washington Bureau Deputy Chief (Time)
Public Affairs Director, EPA (Obama, Trump)	Kelly Zito	Staff Writer (San Francisco Chronicle)
Acting Undersecretary of State (Trump)	Heather Nauert	"Fox and Friends" Host (Fox News)
Communications Dir, WH (Trump)	Anthony Scaramucci	"Wall Street Week" Host (Fox News)
Personal Asst to President, WH (Trump)	John McEntee	Production Assistant (Fox News)
Director, Nat'l Economic Council (Trump)	Larry Kudlow	Sr Contributor (CNBC)
Nat'l Security Advisor, NSC (Trump)	John Bolton	Contributor (Fox News)
Secretary, HUD (Trump)	Ben Carson	Analyst (Fox News)
Comm Dep Chief of Staff, WH (Trump)	Bill Shine	President (Fox News)
Sr Dep Gen Counsel, EPA (Trump)	Erik Baptist	Research Associate (Washington Times)
Public Affairs Assoc Admin, EPA (Trump)	JP Freire	Editor (Washington Examiner)

The Ridiculousness and Illegitimacy of Voting (for Statists) in Obviously Rigged Elections when ½ the Population doesn't even Vote.

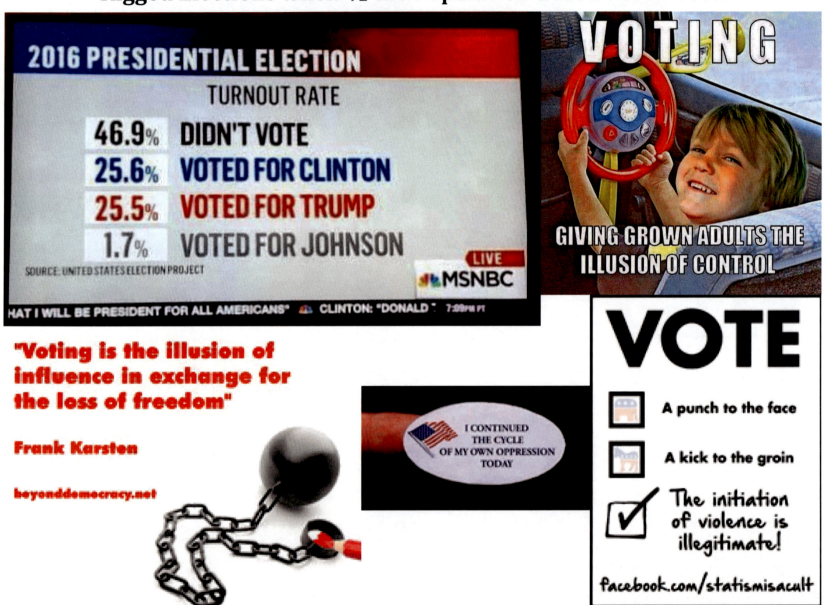

The Ridiculousness and Criminality of the Monopoly Statist Police
(The Increasingly Federalized Domestic Military)

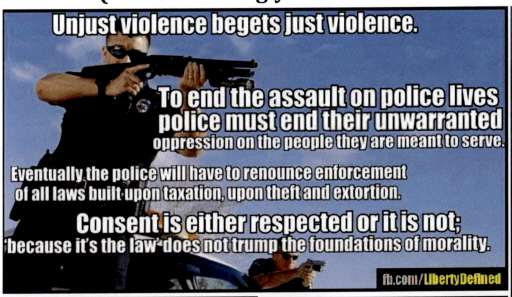
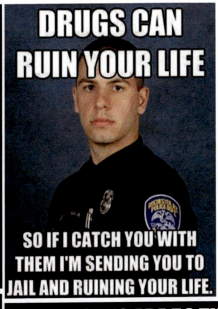

The Ridiculousness and Immorality of the Statist Military

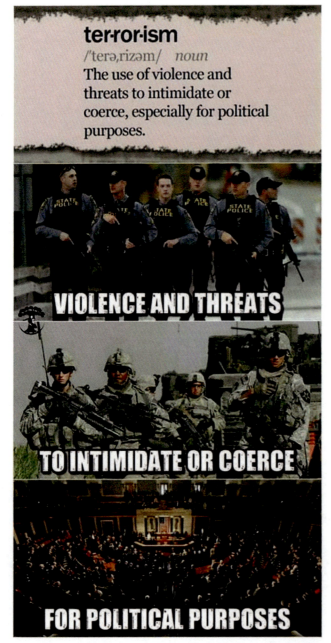

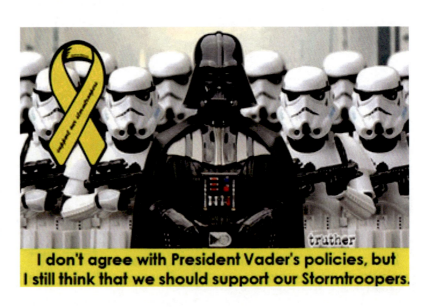

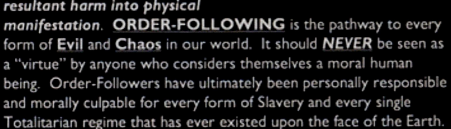

The Incredible Sadness of Mental Slavery

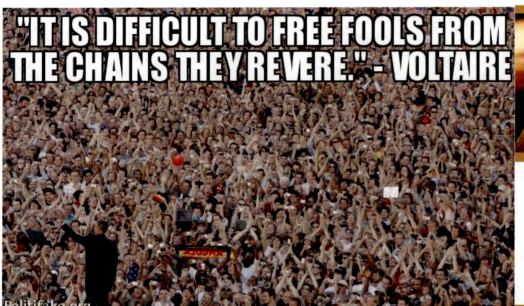

"One of the saddest lessons of history is this: If we've been bamboozled long enough, we tend to reject any evidence of the bamboozle. We're no longer interested in finding out the truth. The bamboozle has captured us. It's simply too painful to acknowledge, even to ourselves, that we've been taken. **Once you give a charlatan power over you, you almost never get it back.**"

Carl Sagan

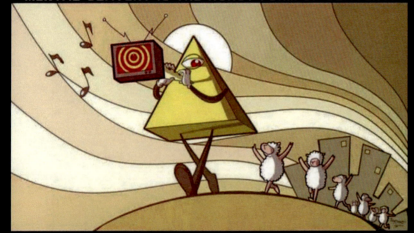

The most effective form of slavery is a system that allows just enough autonomy to give the illusion of freedom, while keeping the public in a perpetual state of indentured servitude.

The Silliness of Statist Arguments Against Voluntaryism/Anarchy

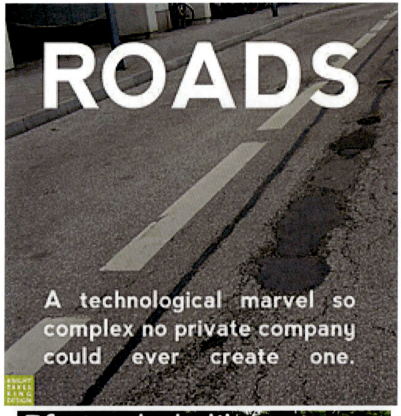

Somalia

"If you don't like government, move to Somalia."

There are several reasons why this is an ignorant thing to say.

1. Somalia is not experiencing anarchy, but anocracy. The problem in Somalia is not a lack of government, but multiple governments, fighting to gain control over the state.
2. Problems in Somalia didn't start with the downfall of the government, they caused the downfall of the government. Somalia was not a prosperous thriving nation before the civil war.
3. There is underlying racism in this line of thought. Somalis are considered to be backwards, incapable of fixing their problems and in general not civilised people.

Solutions

We invite you to read our executive summary

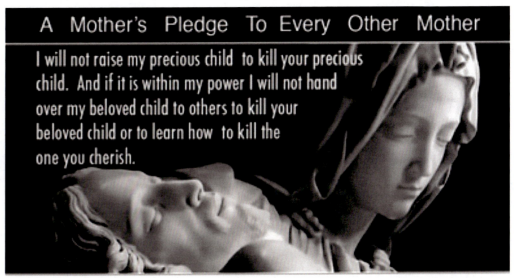

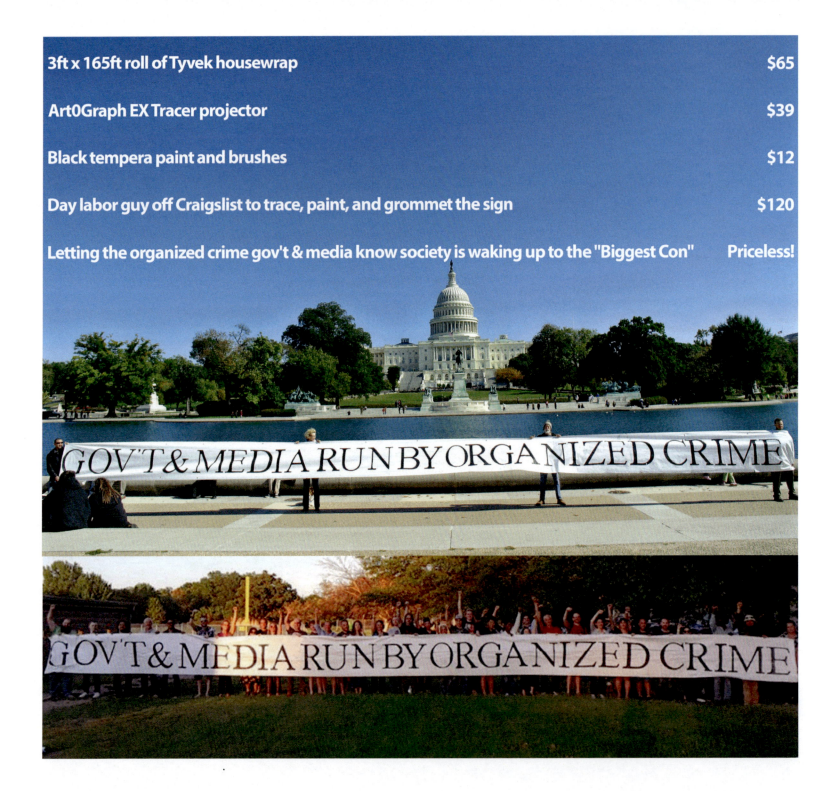

3ft x 165ft roll of Tyvek housewrap	$65
Art0Graph EX Tracer projector	$39
Black tempera paint and brushes	$12
Day labor guy off Craigslist to trace, paint, and grommet the sign	$120
Letting the organized crime gov't & media know society is waking up to the "Biggest Con"	Priceless!

Liberty Hacks - The Easy Substitutions That Make Us Free!

The Good News! There is a Resistance! - For those who are new to this information I know it can be daunting, scary and trigger the psychological defense mechanism of "cognitive dissonance" where the brain simply can't accept new information, even if factual, because it causes pain/fear. Some are even trapped by "Stockholm Syndrome", a well-understood condition where hostages develop a psychological alliance with their captors as a survival strategy during captivity. The Good News? *There is a resistance!* It is growing, picking up speed, only going in one direction and is approaching and capable of exponential growth *if good people get themselves into the fight!* - While we aren't the majority…yet… there is a growing and important "truth movement" that is awakening. While we might not be united on every level we know the system is lying to us and we are coming to some common understandings. Most importantly once people realize there is a "man behind the curtain" in Google/Fedbook/media and/or that government "authority" is *illogical, immoral, indoctrinated and illegitimate* they rarely go back to Statism or wearing a costume/badge that identifies them as an "order-follower" robbing their friends and neighbors. Here are three things that the truth community broadly agrees on and some strategies to *Fight Back!*:

1. The Banks are Stealing the Value Out of Our Money – The ability for banks to create money out of thin air and loan it at interest using a technique called fractional reserve banking they lobbied/bribed Congress to make "legal" with the Federal Reserve Act is making banks trillions while simultaneously stealing the value out of everyone's earnings and savings through inflation. These vast stolen "profits" are what have allowed the banks to control the government and buy up the media companies.

Liberty Hack: Don't do business with the monopoly money center banks especially JP Morgan Chase, Citigroup, Goldman Sachs, Bank of America, HSBC, Barclays, Wells Fargo and UBS. Chose non-affiliated regional banks and credit unions even if it's less convenient.

2. Organized Crime Gov't + Monopoly Media+ CIA Google/Facebook/Twitter = Fake News/Fake "Reality"! - There are 6 Monopoly media companies running hundreds of subsidiaries to offer the illusion of choice but working together as a cartel and using lies, propaganda and unethically manipulative psychological techniques in a coordinated effort to deceive, distract and manipulate society. Google/YouTube/Amazon/Facebook/Wikipedia/Twitter/Reddit/Snopes/Instagram/Pinterest/Drudge Report and others have been caught both promoting false government narratives/views/voices and hiding/lying about alternative narratives/views/facts. The revolution will not be televised or "Recommended for You" by YouTube.

> **Liberty Hack:** *Turn off the Monopoly Media completely* and begin to get your news and information from the developing voices of the alternative media that we recommend in this section. Take the money you are saving from cable television, Netflix, and Amazon Prime and transfer that support to alternative media using donation aggregators like Patreon, Bitbacker.io, , and direct donations.

3. The intelligence agencies and monopoly media are behind "Terrorism" which is designed by *Them* to terrorize *You*! – Multiple "government" intelligence agencies (USA, Israel, Saudi Arabia, Pakistan) behind the 9-11 false flag attacks which transferred trillions to the military-industrial complex and allowed them to steal our civil liberties. FBI & ATF were behind the 1995 Oklahoma City bombing that blew up a day care center to tar the militia movement that was growing rapidly after the FBI Hostage Rescue Team/Delta Force murdered 80 men, women, and children at Waco and then covered it up with the help of the media. FBI and domestic police agencies behind [hundreds of agent provocateured domestic terrorism incidents](#) using low IQ patsies and involvement in suspicious events like: [The Boston Bombing](#), [Sandy Hook](#), the [1993 World Trade Center Car Bomb](#), [Orlando Pulse nightclub shooting](#), and others.

> **Liberty Hack:** *Don't be afraid!* The chances that you or your family will die in an intelligence agency-sponsored false flag terrorist incident or school shooting are quite low, according to one study your chances of being killed by a "terrorist" are 1 in 30,000,000 (vs. killed by the government or police as 1 in 79,815. Focus on the very real danger of shave-headed, mind-controlled government enforcers delusional in the belief they have rights that others don't!

Let's Just Call It Organized Crime - Yes. There was and probably is a Bavarian Illuminati, and there are free masons, dual-citizenship Zionist Israelis, Jesuits, Skull and Bonesmen, Bohemian Grove attendees, Council on Foreign Relations members, Berggruen Institute members, Pilgrim Society, Group of 30 members, Trilaterialists, and Bilderberg group members involved and in key positions of power; if you want to rob the world, you have to have meetings, and it is easy for criminal, monied interests willing to kill, bribe, and blackmail to hijack and control any hierarchical organization over time. But let's not complicate the issue. We can simply refer to the problem as organized crime - because it is. People/the FBI/police understand and can relate to organized crime. Bavarian Illuminati... not so much. Be suspicious of anyone using the amorphous terms: "Globalists", "Elitists", "Deep State" or "New World Order" to describe the problem. These appear to be purposely unhelpful, undescriptive terms.

Accept my sincerest apologies and _then quit working for organized crime_!
I am truly, truly sorry to have to be the one to break this news to you: especially since I have good friends and family who work in the schools, federal/local government, police, military or are veterans. If you shaved your head and wear/ wore a uniform, if you killed because someone told you to, if you locked up peaceful people for victimless crimes, if you inconvenienced travelers and violated their dignity and privacy, if you propagandized and distracted the population from Hollywood, New York, Washington DC, Atlanta, or Langley... **it's OK! You are forgiven**! We are up against an inter-generational, multi-trillion-dollar propaganda, indoctrination, and control system. I went to government schools and was a Cub Scout and a Boy Scout. It took me a while to overcome the programming. I know it is harder to admit the truth if you are drawing a paycheck, but it's time to quit pretending you don't know the government isn't evil, murdering people globally, robbing the population, completely illegitimate on its face and funded by money stolen from others at the point of a gun. If you are in the system and just can't leave...yet... then throw sand in the gears every chance you get: Leak the State's documents, expose the State's crimes, sabotage the State's ability to track, trace and control peaceful people, and *teach the kids in your charge the truth about the system*.

Liberty Hack: *First, flip-the-script! The movement is full of honorable veterans and ex-police officers who signed up to protect their friends, families, and communities and then got out when they realized the truth about "The System". There are hundreds of intelligence officers and military officers/pilots, including Generals and Admirals, who have questioned the official story of 9-11 publicly! Become a scholar, get organized. Many police officers are quitting publicly and speaking out, including Raeford Davis, Barry Cooper, and Brad Jardis.*

Take down or at least replace that flag: It is the symbol of your oppression and an artificial, indoctrinated belief system. You might as well fly the Nazi flag. Same artificial religious symbol. Different sect. We are advocating some version of the Betsy Ross flag (circle of 13 Stars in the blue field) as a protest against organized crime's use of the current flag as an indoctrinated artificial religious symbol. We are suggesting if you are going to fly a flag it should only be in protest to the current "government" and a reminder of America's true glory days where there was essentially no "gubernare mente " / "government", no licenses, no militarized police forces, no fake terrorism, no hoax shooting, no propaganda, no monopolies, no spying, no income tax, no central bank and an essential free market in money! We like our Five Percenter Voluntaryist version!

Forget politics (except for those running to expose and repeal the system): Don't play poker in a crooked card game, and don't vote to rob your friends and neighbors to put your political party's ideas into practice by force. The Libertarian Party appears ineffective with faux-libertarians like Bill Weld and clowns like John McAfee being used to sully it. The only redemption would be a quality candidate running on a platform of a peaceful and orderly dissolution of the federal government and to be NOT-president because the candidate would have the honesty to openly state that political authority is illegitimate. If an honest candidate emerged then the campaign could be used as a referendum on a peaceful and orderly dissolution of the federal government where defense and police powers are transferred to the respective states immediately but under a new ethical natural law-based defensive posture in a model that will need to be ultimately privatized and or managed by a not-for-profit.

Spiritual Health & Wellness

Stay spiritually and physically healthy while detoxing the system's poisons – "The System" loves using its monopoly food and water companies + the "Plug-In Drug" of tell-lie-vision to debilitate the public so they can't think straight, focus and are too sedentary to resist the government or even get off the couch. When you see the sky-rocketing rates of addiction and obesity in the US, blame the drug dealers who are controlling "The System" and their partners in the media who are selling addictive food, beverages, and legal/illegal drugs using a combo of product placement, advertising and monopoly AMA medicine.

Fight Back!: Here are some tips:

Spiritual Health – Get a good night's sleep, try to meditate daily, keep the mind free from negative thoughts and emotions even if someone has wronged you, give everyone the "assumption of good will". Try to stay positive and even *when things go bad realize that you have the ability to control your response*! Spend time in the outdoors and with friends!

Stay Physically Healthy – Try to get physical exercise most days even if you have to get up early, workout during lunch with friends, or hit the gym in the evening. Go vegan! Try to get unfiltered sunlight especially in winter, research sun gazing, get house plants that clean the air, find Doctors that specialize in a holistic and/or Orthomolecular approach focused on nutrition/removing toxins vs. monopoly AMA allopathic medicine that only teaches drug-based therapies. Hot Yoga is a demanding workout, a "moving meditation", and sweating is one of the best detoxification routines available. Research: The Gerson Therapy, Cannabis, and Vitamin B-12 for Cancer over the "Cut, Poison and Burn" of monopoly AMA medicine.

Water – You either use a filter or you are a filter. Drink spring water, distilled and/or Fluoride and Chlorine-free, filtered water where you have the ability to filter yourself. A gravity-fed filter doubles as a portable filter in emergencies but under-the-kitchen-sink-filters and whole house filters are the best for ease-of-use and removing fluoride/chlorine from showering/bathing/swimming water. The Fluoride Action Network has organized thousands of doctors, dentists, scientists, chemists, and environmentalists including both Nobel Prize and Goldman prize winners into a campaign to end water fluoridation because its lowers IQ in children by around 7 IQ points and . Here is brief summary from the organization's website:

> "As of June 2018, a total of 60 studies have investigated the relationship between fluoride and human intelligence, and over 40 studies have investigated the relationship fluoride and learning/memory in animals. Of these investigations, 53 of the 60 human studies have found that elevated fluoride exposure is associated with reduced IQ, while 45 animal studies have found that fluoride exposure impairs the learning and/or memory capacity of animals. The human studies, which are based on IQ examinations of over 15,000 children, provide compelling evidence that fluoride exposure during the early years of life can damage a child's developing brain."

Don't Eat Corporate "Food" or Take Their Addictive Drugs –One shining light is a global clean food revolution that encompasses local-vores, farm-to-plate, know your farmer, Certified GMO-free labeling and back yard gardens. People are figuring out corporate food is toxic food and has frequently been engineered to be addictive using food additives and chemicals including: Glutamates, refined grains, refined sugars, sugar/salt, sugar/fat, etc. From the days of the East India Company, Russell & Company, and the opium trade organized crime has been selling addiction and taking over Big Tobacco, Big Food, and Big Pharma was a logical extension of the addiction-for-profit business model.

Cocaine, Heroin – This is the real reason the US military is currently occupying Afghanistan and both the US Military and DEA are working with the Columbian (Organized Crime) Government in "Plan Columbia". Both are places where the relatively rare poppy is cultivated and processed where they can control the entire area to limit competition.

Legal Opioids & Selective Serotonin Reuptake Inhibitor (SSRIs) drugs- Sackler Family/Purdue Pharma given a government granted monopoly ("Patent") on the "legal" opioid OxyContin which is allowed to be widely overprescribed, prescribed to kids, and even covered by insurance! Purdue has made $35 billion on OxyContin alone since 1996. Other opioids, narcotics and SSRIs given similar government granted monopolies and opioids alone have caused 165,000 deaths since 2000. SSRIs include Prozac, Zoloft, Paxil, Luvox, and Celexa have been linked to, among other issues, suicidal/homicidal ideation and mass shootings.

Injections / Vaccines – It came out in June of 2000 at the CDC's Simpsonwood Meetings that the "government" knew its mandatory vaccinations were causing autism and neurological issues. The government has now admitted that vaccines can cause autism and neurological issues and have paid out billions in their secretive vaccine courts that shield their organized crime pharma partners from liabilities in the regular court system. The 2016 documentary *Vaxxed* features a CDC whistleblower that testifies that the agency lied and destroyed evidence that the MMR vaccine was causing autism and neurological issues.
Best Documentaries: Vaxxed(CDC is lying), The Greater Good(aluminum), and Trace Amounts (mercury)

Sugar – The real "Gateway Drug". Psychologically and physically addictive and added to thousands of food products you would never suspect and even cigarettes whose industry is the #2 user of sugar after food & beverage. Toxic to the body and primes the brain for alcoholism and other forms of addiction.

Tobacco/Nicotine – Tobacco companies add, in some brands, hundreds of additional additives and chemicals that make cigarettes more addictive. According to the U.S. National Cancer Institute: "Of the more than 7,000 chemicals in tobacco smoke, at least 250 are known to be harmful, including hydrogen cyanide, carbon monoxide, and ammonia. Among the 250 known harmful chemicals in tobacco smoke, at least 69 can cause cancer."

Ethyl Alcohol – Liquor, "Spirits", Ale, Beer, Wine. Poisonous to the brain, heavily subliminally marketed (product placement) in television and movies. Blood-sugar imbalances from refined sugar and grains primes for alcoholism.

Caffeine – Addictive, added to soft drinks and energy drinks targeting kids, pre-work out drinks targeting athletes, and with coffee heavily marketed through national monopoly chains Starbucks, Dunkin Donuts, and 7-11 also selling toxic sugar. **Search:** Jason Christoff and Caffeine & 14 Little Known Facts About Coffee

Cannabis – Cannabis can be addictive for some and can blot out emotional pain that is needed for change/healing. Cannabis is being legalized which is good. Much less harmful than alcohol but often sold by the organized crime's "government" shops or politically connected licensees. Better to use the black market then give organized crime a nickel. Watch out for genetically modified "Monsanto" cannabis, toxic pesticides and strains designed and widely distributed to achieve couch-lock in front of the tell-lie-vision.

Television/Internet/Gaming addiction – The "Plug-In Drug" – Think of the television, gaming, social media and internet video as weapon platforms to steal your time, deceive you, or capture your attention long enough to show you a commercial usually for something addictive, harmful or, during the political season, to trick you into participating in organized crime's puppet show. The medium itself elicits a state of "attentional inertia," marked by lowered activity in the part of the brain that processes complex information. Television exploits human psychology to keep people glued to the set using, among other techniques, human's biological pre-disposition to watch high-status monkeys I.E. "Celebrities", sexually attractive people, and the brain's survival mechanism of tracking constant motion. YouTube both censors algorithmically and tempts you with time-wasters to distract you away from doing anything that would lead you out of slavery.

Meat – Humans are biologically herbivores and can reduce their incidents of obesity, cholesterol, and other health issues by ditching meat. The blood in meat contains albumin, hemoglobin and gamma globulin and all of these chemicals activate opioid receptors. When meat eaters were treated with a drug used to block opiate receptors, ham consumption fell by 10%, salami by 25% and tuna by 50%!
Best Documentaries: What the Health?, Dominion And The Game Changers.

Dairy – Humans are the only species that drinks milk past adolescence or the milk of another species even though 75% of the population is lactose intolerant because our bodies aren't designed to process it. Casein, one of the proteins in milk, crosses the blood-brain barrier and becomes something called casomorphins. Which sounds a lot like morphine—because casomorphin is also an opioid.

Glutamates – a class of food additive best known for Monosodium Glutamate (MSG) but includes glutamates deceptively hidden by the addiction industry as: yeast extract, textured protein, whey protein, soy protein, and dozens of other tricky names and derivatives to make food physically and psychologically addictive.

Culture War

Turn off the bought-and-paid-for Mainstream Media and begin getting your news and information from the authentic voices on the self-directed Internet.

Alternative News Frequencies: The Corbett Report YouTube /Podcast, Tragedy & Hope, The Anti-Media, Press for Truth (Canada), Technocracy News and Trends, Mint Press News, Global Research

Voluntaryist and libertarian political commentaries: Larken Rose Website/YouTube, Mark Passio - Website / YouTube, Ernest Hancock - Freedom's Phoenix, Pirates without Borders, and Declare Your Independence radio show, Brian Young -HighImpactFlix – Truth videos, Carey Wedler, Max Igan, The Free Thought Project, CopBlock, Liberty.me / Jeffrey Tucker (Chief Liberty Officer), The Pholosopher, LewRockwell.com, MediaMonarchy, Pete "Mance Rayder" Raymond.

Researchers and Organizations Focused on Government and Media Corruption: Institute for the Study of Globalization & Covert Politics, Light On Conspiracies (Ole Dammegard), False Flag Weekly News, Memory Hole Blog (Professor James Tracy), Jim Fetzer, Whitney Webb, Plasmaburns, MrStosh (Censored off the net?), Douglas Valentine (CIA crimes)

Musical Artists: Truniversal - introspective hip-hop and spoken word, DISL Automatic – Truth hop with a message, Jordan Page – acoustical guitar, Eric July/Backwordz, Rob Hustle – Triple threat, Neema V.- Hip Hop & Dub Plates, Alais Clay, The Wandering Monks, Freedom Movement, Remo Conscious, Tatiana Moroz, The Founders – Anarchist Hardcore Metal

Healers and Life Facilitators: Kenny Palurintano – Travelling Vegan Chef and life facilitator, BurntMD – aKa: The Guerrilla Healer, Bernhard Guenther – Integrative Bodywork & Holistic Coaching, Clive de Carle, Jason Christoff

Voluntaryist Anarchist Comedy (YouTube Sensations): Benny Wills/Kevin Kostelnik = Joy Camp, Remy Munasifi (YouTube), Doug Stanhope, Comic Dave Smith, and George Carlin

Facebook Groups and Meme Creators: AnarchyBall (Facebook), The *Art* of Liberty Foundation, Statism is Still a Cult,

Shooting, Physical Security & Combat Arms: Max Velocity Tactical

Technology & Information Security Researchers: Richard Stallman, RestorePrivacy.com, privacytools.io, Free Software Foundation, Techrights

Avoid Untrustworthy Frequencies: Anyone pumping Trump, Tulsi, Bernie, Bloomberg, Elizabeth, AoC, Cory Booker, or any other tell-a-vision manufactured government savior or casino-owning "outsider" is suspect. Anyone promoting communism, socialism, fascism, neoconservatism, "democracy" or any other government system that is easily hijacked and controlled by monied interests is at best misguided and worst a paid political agitator or agent. Let me know if any of our trusted frequencies are suspect. Yes, Alex Jones is a tool/gatekeeper. The Drudge Report is designed to waste your time with click-bait and keep you in the fake left/right Statist paradigm. If it is coming from a MainStreamMedia company or being pushed/"suggested for you" by Google News, YouTube, Facebook, Reddit, Wikipedia, Snopes, or other "control-of-perception" media companies it is automatically suspect!

Untrusted Frequencies & Probable Controlled Opposition (Partial List): DrudgeReport, InfoWars, Liberty Hangout, Edward Snowden, Joe Rogan, David Icke, QAnon, Russel Brand, Jessie Ventura, Vice News, Noam Chomsky, Stefan Molyneux, Paul Joseph Watson, Democracy Now, The Young Turks, Glenn Beck, Your News Wire, Christopher Cantwell, Millie Weaver, Kaitlin Bennett and Owen Shroyer

Take Back and (Ultimately) Privatize the Government School System

Remove Your Kids from the government indoctrination system: I would rather my children be uneducated than be educated by the State. Government schools are designed to slave-up and dumb-down your kids. Everything about the government school system is wrong: segregation by age vs. ability, the compulsory pledge of allegiance, and the use of collective punishment, corporal punishment, and public shaming as obedience techniques. Red/Yellow/Green classroom management techniques, restrictions on movement without permission, lack of freedom to use the restroom without permission, mandatory vaccinations, searches, school "resource officers", sex education, death education, whole language, D.A.R.E. Programs, surveillance cameras, active shooter drills, ineffective teaching methodologies (whole language, common core, standardized tests to name a few) and indoctrinating kids into a hidden religion: Statism.

Fight Back!: *Take Your Kids Out of the Government's "Schools"* - It is much better to use private schooling, homeschooling, or <u>unschooling</u>, especially if your kids are old enough to learn auto-didactically and are capable of self-directed learning or apprenticeship focused on their interests. Check out <u>Autonomy</u> as an alternative

Organize a Petition and Town Hall Meeting in Your Community to Expose and Mitigate These Techniques– We have a <u>petition template demanding that the government schools take Statism and militarism out of the schools</u> that you are free to use or modify. We suggest using the petition process to promote a town hall meeting with invited experts to explain Statism, the hidden obedience techniques and the dangers of the government's mandatory shots. Please contact me at <u>UoSlavery@ProtonMail.com</u> to see if I am available. At the meeting arm up concerned parents with information & the petition and schedule another town hall meeting several weeks out and invite the local school board, present the completed petition, and have an open conversation on their use of statism, obedience techniques and the need to ultimately privatize their services.

Understand the Hidden Curriculum of Mandatory Government Schools: If you still believe you need to have your kids in school then understand the hidden curriculum and help your kids to understand and question the immorality and illogic of Statism. Explain and push back on the obedience techniques being used against them.

1. Statism- the indoctrinated belief in the necessity, desirability and legitimacy of government. I.E. How to be a slave and submit to organized crime's control system. The common prayer of the pledge of allegiance and the national anthem, You're an "American".. It's been decided for you!

2. Obedience to authority/government - Subtle unethically manipulative techniques used in the mandatory schools include conditioning kids to governmental "authority" from a young age: can't leave their seat without gov't permission, red, yellow, green troublemaker boards, warrantless searches, see-through backpacks, metal detectors, corporal punishment, collective punishment, Pavlovian drill bells, Police officers in schools, scouting and jROTC Uniforms, repetition, D.A.R.E. program, and Statism.

3. Debilitation – Purposely crappy and morality-free education, No focus on the Trivium: Logic, Grammar and Rhetoric. Mandatory mercury and aluminum-laced vaccines, frequently toxic corporate processed foods made with refined grains, refined sugars, Glyphosate and glutamates, rBGH in dairy, and Fluoridated water linked to lower IQ in 50+ studies in the water fountain.

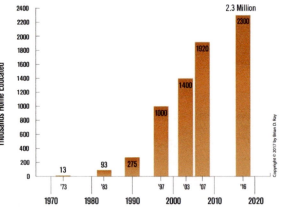

Some of What the School System Is Hiding:

Libertarianism/Voluntaryism – Not everyone believes in "Government/ Gubernare Mente" (Organized Crime) and you don't really owe "Government" or anyone else any money or allegiance because of where you were born. "Government" schools are echo chamber church schools where everyone who has wised up to the scam has been quietly moving their kids to private schools, parochial schools or homeschooling them leaving only the "true believers".

Government Criminality – Whether or not you believe in having a government, the government's mandatory school system and rip-off universities have been hiding/minimizing government's obvious lies and crimes: From the fraud and inflationary theft of fractional reserve banking to the CIA's murderous history of Phoenix Program death squads and drug dealing to trillions transferred to private banks and media companies through the TARP/TALF and "Bailouts" to the actuarial impossibility of social security.

Fight Back!: We are suggesting organizing with other students and parents to demand an end to the most obviously unethically manipulative Statist/Militarist and obedience techniques.

1. Talk with Teacher(s) and Administrators – Discuss requests and demands with teachers. Some suggestions: No pledge of allegiance, No militarism, no Red, Yellow, Green "Classroom Management Techniques", No D.A.R.E. program, no school resource officers, no searches, No assigned seating, no active shooter drills, , No walking in lines, no control of movement, and **no mandatory vaccinations!**

2. Privatization: Have an open discussion on the need to ultimately privatize operations. Because there can be no legitimate government there can be no government-funded schools. Teachers and administrators need to begin thinking about how they will privatize school operations and compete for students in a competitive free market. An obvious model would be a transitional year where each individual school knows it will need to plan for and attract paying students, donations from alumni, and a new business model with teachers getting the freedom to set their own curriculum, rates, co-teaching partnerships, and administrators having to compete for both teachers and students.

3. Organize Petitions & Town Hall Meetings – Rent a hall, organize experts to speak, print flyers/petitions and distribute them in your neighborhood. Bake cookies, get together with friends, Make it fun to resist!

4. Rock-Star Level - Organize an on-going maker-space/co-working space for freedom similar to Freedom's Phoenix in Arizona, the Liberty Lodge in Denver, the Praxeum in Portsmouth, and The Quill in Manchester!

Resources from The Liberator in the Folder: The Hidden Curriculum of Mandatory Government Schools
The Hidden Curriculum of Compulsory Schooling - **John Taylor Gatto**
The Underground History of American Education, Volume I: An Intimate Investigation Into the Prison of Modern Schooling - **John Taylor Gatto**
Dumbing Us Down - **John Taylor Gatto**

Boycott, divest & buy local/small: Break the chains! Economic boycott and divestment are your strongest weapons: Don't buy from the banker's monopoly companies! Don't pay for their movies, games, and entertainment. Even though you can get anything you want from a mason in two days with free shipping… DON'T… If you can avoid it.

Amason Appears to be Part of Organized Crime's Control-of-Perception Program
Amason has been caught digitally burning books on their "Kindle" and "Fire" platforms, censoring books exposing the Sandy Hook hoax, 9-11 Truth, engineered Islamic mass migration in Europe, and other government criminality, censoring book reviews including negative reviews of Hillary Clinton's book "What Happened". Amason Prime removed the award winning documentary *Vaxxed* which exposed that the CDC has been lying about vaccines causing autism, other vaccine-awareness videos including *Shoot-Em Up- The Truth About Vaccines*, and *Man Made Epidemic*. They have also censored *Flipping the Script: When Parents Fight Back* (harmfulness of chemotherapy for kids), *Root Causes* (Harmfulness of root canals), *Behind the Fear: The Hidden Story of HIV* (HIV Scam) & *Cancer Can Be Killed* (how to cure cancer naturally). Amason Prime (and Netflix with their $50M deal with the Obamas) are the prime outlets for the 800+ movies and 1000+ television shows funded/supported by the DoD and intelligence agencies that are product-placing the American flag, making government employees (FBI/CIA/ATF/Police,etc.) the heroes, and using propaganda techniques like anchoring where scenes of high positive emotion are created and then "anchored" to the flag.

Amason Getting Hundreds of Millions from the Intelligence Agencies and Spying on the Population with Alexa, Echo and Ring Cameras

Amason has a $600 million dollar deal with the intelligence agencies for secure cloud services and other agencies spend more than $47 million a year for cloud services alone. Amason (supposedly) lost a $10 Billion dollar DoD contract for the JEDI "war cloud" network but they are appealing the decision so don't be surprised when organized crime gets handed more tax payer dollars.
Amason's Alexa and Echo spy on the population in their homes and the company' Ring Doorbell cameras have been quietly wired into over 600+ police departments (and likely Homeland Security Fusion Centers) to create a network of surveillance cameras in suburban neighborhoods that never would have been tolerated if the organized crime government had done so openly. The Amason Key system puts a camera in your house covering everyone coming and going and lets them remotely unlock the door.

Could Amazon be a front company for organized crime designed to monopolize online retail, censor, and digitally "burn" books on the Kindle and Fire?

UnderstandingOurSlavery.com/amazon

Amason's Economic Warfare Against Its Own Customers and the Population

In addition to control-of-perception and spying, Amason is now openly competing with its own customers: The company's third-party marketplace represents millions of individual sellers who sell on the Amason platform (including this author to get the evidence out before we are censored off). Amason began competing with their customers in 2009 with their own private label brands. As of August 2019 the company had 135 private label brands ranging from baby food to camera supplies to groceries, up from 80 private label brands in June of 2018 with an additional 330 "exclusive brands" manufactured by a 3rd party but only sold on Amason. Many intelligent observers believe Amason was financed by the organized crime banks and "government" to destroy mom & pop retail and individual mail order sellers in a program to destroy private wealth so the population doesn't have the resources to resist organized crime's take-over and keeps them working constantly without the time to research and understand the slavery system. The "government's" exorbitant income and property taxes, estate taxes, hidden taxes, monopoly privileges, inflation and endless warfare are other examples of the same criminal policy.

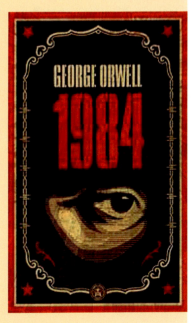

"The problem was how to keep the wheels of industry turning without increasing the real wealth of the world. Goods must be produced, but they need not be distributed. And in practice the only way of achieving this was by continuous warfare.

... The essential act of war is destruction, not necessarily of human lives, but of the products of human labor. War is a way of shattering to pieces, our pouring into the stratosphere, or sinking into the depths of the sea, materials which might otherwise be used to make the masses too comfortable, and hence in the long run, too intelligent...

...In principle the war effort is always so planned as to eat up any surplus that might exist after meeting the bare needs of the population. In practice the needs of the population are always underestimated, with the result being that there is a chronic shortage of half the necessities of life; this is looked upon as an advantage. It is deliberate policy to keep even the favored groups somewhere near the brink of hardship, because a general state of scarcity increases the importance of small Privileges and thus magnifies the distinction between one group and another."

Socialist dictator Emmanuel Goldstein's description of the real reason for warfare in George Orwell's book **1984** which Amason digitally burned on their "Kindle" and sent down "the memory hole".

Get Together and Get Concentrated

Get concentrated - Support & move to voluntaryist and libertarian communities:
Libertarians are organizing all over the world in various efforts to secure an area with political sovereignty to implement societies free from the control system of "government". The largest and most exciting is the Free State Project, an effort that has organized over 24,000+ activists who have pledged to move to New Hampshire and campaign actively for its political independence. The group has already moved and organized over 5,000 in the state with more arriving every week and has spent over a decade successfully rolling back laws, getting libertarians elected to office, and building the political and social networks needed for societal change. I believe if we free New Hampshire then we, ultimately, win everywhere. Think about concentrating some of your "firepower" (activism, resources, investment) in New Hampshire including coming out for one of the FSP's engaging events:

FSP New Hampshire Liberty Events: PorcFest - Porcupine Freedom Festival every June, the Freecoast Festival (Sept, Portmouth) or the Liberty Forum (February, Manchester), Free State Blockchain Digital Asset Conference (October, Portsmouth)

Other Global Voluntaryist and Liberty Communities:
Europe: Liberland (Serbia/Croatia border, Europe), Liberstad (Norway),

Central/South America and Caribbean: Fort Galt (Chile), The Anarchists of Acapulco (Mexico), Cheran (Mexico) The town that kicked out the "government"

Other: Seasteading Institute - the oceans, The Floating Island Project (French Polynesia) The Free Society and Free Private Cities - Are attempts to negotiate political sovereignty similar to or within an existing Special Economic Zone (Country TBD) Caledonia - represents individuals who share the common value of adherence to the non-aggression principle, and who voluntarily agree to associate for the purposes of trade, mutual aid, arbitration, defense against all aggressors, regardless of their claims of authority, and the preservation of wealth via stable inflation-proof currencies.

Free State Project (FSP) FSP.org & facebook.com/groups/TheFreeStateProject/	Organizing 20,000+ new movers to move to New Hampshire and activate for Liberty
FSP Welcome Wagon https://www.facebook.com/groups/FSPWelcomeWagon/	Organizes move-in parties to help new movers unload for free. You supply the pizza and the beer.
FSP Jobs Board https://www.facebook.com/groups/fspjobalert/	Active job board to help FSP movers and potential movers find work in New Hampshire.
The Pre-State Project https://understandingourslavery.com/home-2/foundation/	Organizing 25,000 "Pre-Staters" (liberty advocates already in New Hampshire) to support the Free State Project & other NH liberty orgs.
Granite Logic – A Liberty Oriented Book Exchange https://www.granitelogic.org/	Objectivist reading club that stocks liberty-oriented book exchange mini-libraries in public places.
New Hampshire Liberty Alliance https://nhliberty.org & facebook.com/NHLiberty/	A nonpartisan, libertarian coalition in NH. They supports libertarian candidates for state/local offices & rate legislation.
Foundation for New Hampshire Independence nhindependence.org	Educate citizens on the benefits of NH peacefully declaring its independence and separating from the federal government.
New Hampshire Exit - #NHExit NHExit.com & facebook.com/groups/1056520281105982/	Hashtag & movement for NH independence and secession from the organized crime federal government.
Health Freedom NH facebook.com/groups/healthfreedomnh/ Mailing List: eepurl.com	Local and grassroots group, challenging ourselves and our communities to improve health and freedom.
Human Action Foundation & The Praxeum – **A liberty community center in Dover, NH** https://humanaction.foundation/	Promote flourishing communities of freethinkers. We provide educational events, charitable services, and infrastructure to communities in which we operate.
Liberty.Menu & The FSP Calendar https://www.fsp.org/calendar/ https://www.Liberty.Menu	Liberty Menu is a NH (and national!) directory of liberty events, businesses, and media creators. The FSP calendar lists 550+ liberty oriented NH Meet-ups.

Liberty Events

Event Name	Month/Date	Location
Free State Project's Liberty Forum	February 1&2, 2020	Manchester, NH
Phoenix Freedom Summit	February 7&8, 2020	Phoenix, AZ
Anarchapulco	February 10-20, 2020	Acapulco, Mexico
The *Art* of Liberty on the Beach (The Turtle Party)	Feb 14th, 2020	Bonfil Beach, Acapulco
Mid-Continent Liberty Festival(MidFest)	April 11&12, 2020	Tahlequah, OK
Anarchizona	March	Sedona, AZ
Libre Planet - Free Software Foundation's Conf	March 14th & 15th	Cambridge, MA
Porcupine Freedom Festival	June 22nd-27th	New Hampshire
Freedom Fest	July 13-16, 2020	Las Vegas, NV
AnarchoVegas	July 19, 2020	Las Vegas, NV
Rainbow Gathering	July 1-7, 2020	TBD-Idaho
The Jackalope Freedom Festival	July/August	Baca Meadows, AZ
Midwest Peace and Liberty Fest	August	Michigan
AnarCon	August 14-16, 2020	Richmond, VA
The Freecoast Festival	September	Portsmouth, NH

Get together: Meet others, have fun, and get involved: **State By State**: **Arizona:** Greater Phoenix Mutual Aid and Safety Society **Colorado:** Denver – We Are Change, **New Hampshire**: Free State Project, Portsmouth-The Praxeum, **Texas:** Houston Free Thinkers, Voluntaryist of Austin **Virginia** - Liberate Richmond, New York Anarcho-Capitalist Meet up, Bay Area Voluntaryists, London Anarchy Meetup, Libertarian Free Thinkers of Kansas City, Voluntaryists of Dallas/Fort Worth, Caledonia (everywhere)

Preparedness and Crypto-Currencies

Prepare for the worst: Because the gov't, the markets, and the dollar have been managed by organized crime for so long, the mafia's political puppets have, of course, looted the nation.

The U.S. economy is starting to smell like a Ponzi scheme in which bankers give themselves the ability to create money out of thin air using fractional reserve banking and where they have attempted to buy the world with their rapidly depreciating fiat-paper tickets. The "government" is on the hook for $23 trillion in debt and unfunded liabilities between $75-200+ trillion. Social Security is actuarially insolvent, the system has been raided, and trillions of dollars in government IOUs are left. The Pentagon can't account for over $10 trillion, the US Postal Service has lost over $57 Billion dollars over the past decade, and Amtrak claims it lost $834 million in 10 years on food and beverage alone, and local, State, and Federal pension schemes are underfunded by 5 Trillion, looted, and/or mismanaged. The government's illegitimacy and criminality are being exposed, and cryptocurrencies, community currencies, barter, and agorism are starting to challenge the economic system. Don't be surprised when the Ponzi scheme collapses.

Diversify into and use cryptocurrencies + barter + commodity money + community currencies: The better you and your community are diversified into $USD alternatives, the more resilient you will be against a dollar collapse or devaluation. We like beans, bullets, and Band-Aids as your core wealth. After the basics, we like community currencies and precious metals in small denominations of a recognizable hallmark. Then, monetary metals stored in other jurisdictions but instantly spendable and transferable. After that, non-inflationary, anonymous cryptocurrencies that promote privacy and digital liberty.

We like cryptocurrency but are realists with respect to its potential for good or evil.

Crypto-Savages Beware! The NSA was thinking Crypto in 1996!

The US National Security Agency (NSA), whose primary job seems to be spying on their friends and neighbors, published a technical white paper entitled: How to Make a Mint: The Cryptography of Anonymous Electronic Cash in June of 1996 outlining a blockchain-based cryptographically secure digital currency and digital "wallet" 12 years before Satoshi Nakamoto published his whitepaper. So it's very possible that Bitcoin was created by the CIA/NSA (**N**akamoto, **SA**toshi to make them: "shine" I.E. Take Satoshi's e-mail: Satoshin@gmx.com add/duplicate the "N" to the front and you get="NSA-to-Shin@"gmx.com and Satoshi Nakamoto is loosely translated to "Central Intelligence" in Japanese. Additionally, Cryptocurrencies have all the hallmarks of intelligence agency, Wall Street/Banking, and Hollywood manipulation with early entrants & manufactured moguls having ties to Hollywood (Brock Pierce), banking/MIC-connected firms like Goldman Sachs (Joe Lubin), SAIC, Raytheon, Boeing, and Northrup Grumman (Larimers) among others.

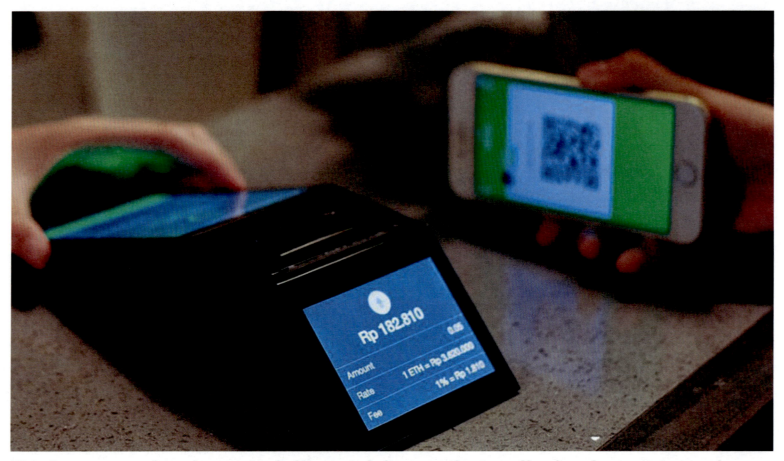

Bitcoin appears to have been crippled purposely by some faction of bankers by scooping up the core development team with $55M in venture cap lead by AXA Strategic Ventures whose parent company AXA is headed by Bilderberg Chairman Henri de Castries. AXA/Blockstream maneuvered the coin away from its original design which sent the fees and transaction times to levels that crippled key features like microtransactions, remittances, and its use as a cash alternative. The market is developing other alternatives for digital cash including: Bitcoin Cash and Dash with some coins like Monero, Grin and Z-Cash displaying anonymity features that are desirable but always vulnerable to Hegelian Dialectic **Problem-Reaction-Solution – Problem**: Bitcoin is the obviously bankster-hijacked compliance crypto, Manage the inevitable: **Reaction**(Freedom activists dump Bitcoin) = Attempt to steer Reaction towards pre-selected **Solution:** the mark-of-the-beast-turn-off-ability-to-buy-and-sell-crypto-currency which was the Banker's plot all-along. There is no completely trusted anonymous crypto yet!

The Bitcoin eco-system is being steered toward Segregated Witness (Segwit) and the Lightning Network, both of which destroy privacy features and create hooks into the conventional banks and payment processors. LocalBitcoins.com, which use to facilitate anonymous in-person transactions now requires Know Your Customer (KYC) while the anonymous in-person transactions have moved over to Bitcoin Cash @ Local.Bitcoin.com

Radio Personality Ernest Hancock is setting the standard for what the voluntaryist community expects out of anonymous digital currency with his [2nd Letter of Captain Marque](#):

> *"A digital economy... requires a new currency that is peer-to-peer, without third party observation, that can be exchanged using an encrypted signal. It must combine the solidity of precious materials, and the fluidity of digital information. We must move funds further, faster and cheaper than ever before, and make decisions based on an ever-accelerating flow of information. So, pirates require virtually instantaneous transactions, with no arbitrary limits on volume, or artificial influences on fees.*
> *Most importantly, a pirate currency must preclude centralization. It must endure as a decentralized network in the face of an adversary that wishes to crimp it into service. Otherwise it will become another link in our chain to the Crown. Given the choice, a superior will result in the obsolescence of the coin of the realm, and the extinction of the Crown itself."*

Freedom Apps, Blockchain, and Crypto Projects for Digital Liberty

Flash Drives - We think the most important freedom app is the flash drive. With the organized crime government and their cartel companies now openly censoring search results on Google, YouTube, Reddit, Wikipedia, and other video and social media platforms, Amazon beta-testing digitally burning books on their "Kindle" and "Fire" platforms, and DARPA openly researching how to use AI to widely censor and takedown content, videos, and even websites, having a back-up of the evidence of "government" and media criminality and the best books and documentaries on the ideas of liberty is crucial.

The Liberator - www.Government-Scam.com/Liberator - The *Art* of Liberty Foundation's collection of 8GB flash drives and Dropboxes that both expose the organized crime's illegitimacy, illogic and criminality and provide the healthy alternatives or voluntaryism, free markets, tolerance, and peace. The Liberator drives includes the PDF of *Understanding Our Slavery* with active links of this book and a curated curriculum of the best books, short videos, and documentaries to take someone from "0-60" on the most important topics in the world.

"Pirate Box" / "Freedom Box "Wifi File Servers - A "Pirate Box"/"Freedom Box" is a portable wi-fi end-point with its own power source that broadcasts a custom Wi-fi SSID but when users attach to the end-point they get a message board and the ability to download files vs. wi-fi. They can be used in organized crime courthouses (Example SSID: "Juror Info" to broadcast jury nullification information to ensure that jurors understand they can judge the law and not just the facts of the case to throw out victimless crimes. We have an *Art* of Liberty Foundation donor that has donated $1000 to put up 10 Pirate Boxes in New Hampshire "Government schools" that would broadcast the SSID: "What the Government School is Hiding From You" and when kids connect they can download this book and the files from our flash drive/Dropbox of Freedom: The Liberator. We are currently looking for articulate Junior/Senior students with gravitas to be ambassadors for Liberty in their schools capable of taking a 1st amendment stand against potential censorship. Please e-mail us at UoSlavery@ProtonMail.com if you know the right student.

Untrustworthy Service, App or Provider	Caught Censoring/Abusing Power? Examples:	Alternative Service, App or Provider	Overview
911- Monopoly Government Police	Work for organized crime, Live on money stolen from others, road piracy, kidnapping and extortion for victimless crimes, and asset forfeiture. untrustworthy and likely to shoot your dog.	**Cell 411** getcell411.com	Set up your Five (V) group, freedom cell, or friends/family with Cell 411 and have trusted friends get notified to respond to emergencies including when the criminals are cops.
Google Search Engine	CIA Google caught manipulating search results, auto-complete to control perception. Liberator Article: *How the CIA Made Google* exposes DARPA funding and control. Project Veritas whistleblower Zach Voorhies exposed blacklists & criminality.	**DuckDuckGo** www.duckduckgo.com/ **Swisscows** SwissCows.ch **Dogpile** www.dogpile.com	DuckDuckGo and Swisscows claim not to monitor/retain search results. Dogpile is meta-browsers that query multiple search engines.
Gmail	CIA Google caught scanning Gmail accounts to target ads, reserves right to read e-mails to deal with " a bug or abuse"	**Your Own Mail Server - BEST** **ProtonMail** ProtonMail.com	ProtonMail is an open-source, freemium e-mail with end-to-end encryption that doesn't spy on you.
Google Docs Google Calendar	Google caught manipulating search results, auto-complete to control perception. Liberator Article: *How the CIA Made Google* exposes DARPA funding and control.	**Zoho Docs** Zoho.com Zoho Calendar	Zoho is an Indian software company that offers cloud-based productivity apps similar to Google Docs and Microsoft Office.
Google Chrome	Google Chrome tracks user activity, automatically signs you into CIA Google to track you and remains open to cookies by default.	**Brave Browser** brave.com/eti875 **Mozilla Firefox** https://www.mozilla.org	Brave- Faster than Chrome and built on the open-source Chromium standard so you can use extensions for Chrome.
Snopes	Organizations that have busted Snopes for lying: Dr. Mercola, Food Babe, Wash. Times,	**Trive** trive.news Start-up, raising funds	Decentralized fact checking using game theory and reputation engines to prevent gaming the system.
Microsoft Windows	Known backdoors. Mircrosoft is in the governments back pocket. Tons of security holes. Anti-virus protection is a must. Proprietary source code.	**Linux Mint** linuxmint.com recommended edition: Cinnimon	Linux Mint is an open source alternative to Mirosoft Windows & Mac OS. Linux Mint is surprisingly easy to setup and use. slight learning curve. Viruses almost non existent.
Microsoft Office (Word, Excel, PowerPoint)	Cost and proprietary code issues and you are giving Microsoft money.	**Libre Office** libreoffice.org **MailSpring** MailSpring.com	Libre Office is free and open source alternative to Mirosoft Office. Robust and is compatible with MS Office docs. Windows/Mac/Linux.

Untrustworthy Service, App or Provider	Caught Censoring/Abusing Power? Examples:	Alternative Service, App or Provider	Overview
YouTube	Owned by CIA Google. Caught ; censoring videos, demonetizing political videos, and not indexing truth videos on the site.	**BitChute** BitChute.com **153News.net** 153News.net **LBRY** lbry.com	BitChute is a peer-to-peer video torrent site. 153news.net is a video sharing site that doesn't censor and where videos can be downloaded from the site.
Facebook	Facebook appears to be a "rebranded" DARPA project called LifeLog has been caught censoring political speech, banning alternative media organizations, and manipulating emotions.	Pocketnet.app Isegoria.com Flote.app, Steemit.com Minds.com, MeWe.com	Open source social media alternatives
Twitter	Twitter "shadow bans" political speech, and at least one key executive has been outed as a British psychological warfare officer.	**Mastadon** Mastadon.social	Mastadon.social is a decentralized, open source social media platform with option to run your own server.
Disqus Comment engine for websites	Disqus has been caught censoring political speech and is in partnership with Google's Jigsaw to use AI to censor comments.	**WordPress Comment Plug-In**	
MeetUp	Caught censoring the #Unrig campaign and our own Etienne de la Boetie2 account. Owned by obviously criminal WeWork	**GetTogether** gettogether.community **City Socializer** citysocializer.com	Open source alternative to MeetUp.
Amazon (A Mason?) Kindle & Fire eBook Platforms	Amazon reached into customer's Kindle eBook readers in 2009 and made copies of 1984 go down the memory hole in what smells like a beta test to digitally burn books in the future. "Kindle" & "Fire".. Get it?	Undeletable Paper Books Please contribute trusted alternatives on our Freedom Apps, Crypto and Blockchain Trello Board for the next edition.	
Amazon (A Mason?) Ring Doorbells	Amazon has video-sharing partnerships with over 400 police forces (likely shared with Federal "Fusion Centers") creating a network of surveillance cameras in suburban neighborhoods	Please contribute trusted alternatives on our Freedom Apps, Crypto and Blockchain Trello Board for the next edition.	
Google Drive MS OneDrive	Microsoft and Google are untrustworthy companies. See above	**SynchThing** syncthing.net	Open source, decentralized alternative for file back up and synch.

Hardware Solutions - Computing and Mobile Phones

Puri-sm - **Librem** are the first high-end linux-based laptops and smartphones where the owner is in control and have complete visibility into the operating system, all bundled software, and the deeper levels of the computer with hardwire switches to turn-off the microphone and camera.

Neuron GhostPads - Custom laptops with the Intel Management Engine disabled and open source trusted software.

Encrypted & Uncensorable Communications - Because organized crime "governments" are spying on their populations the same way the Nazis, Russians and East Germany Stasi did (which is another proof of criminality) it is important to shield your communications through encryption. All communications apps running on Apple IOS, Android and Microsoft devices remain vulnerable to the operating systems being compromised and the device being "screen scrapped" before encryption/transmission or after decryption at the receiving end.

Signal - Encrypted messaging for android, iOS and Desktop.

Telegram - Encrypted messaging for android, IOS, and web. Client apps are open source but there server side is not yet but promised. Ability to run large group chats.

Keybase - Secure groups, chats, and file managment where every account has a built-in crypto wallet (lumens) and the ability to cross-verify your identity to other accounts and websites that you control.

Maskbook - Browser plug-in that encrypts your posts and chats on Facebook to keep them from Facebook (Beta Product).

Tessercube – OpenPGP for mobile devices

Tor Browser - Warning: Developed by Navy & NSA rumored to populate xit nodes

Completely Untrusted: Facebook Messenger, WhatsApp - Owned by Fedbook

Operating System & Computing Alternatives -

Microsoft Windows, Google Android, and Apple IOS are untrusted operating systems. Edward Snowden released **NSA slides mocking Apple iPhone users for giving them their** data and revealing that **the NSA has direct access into Microsoft, Google, Yahoo, YouTube and Apple**.

Debian - Free and open source non-Windows/Apple OS

Tails - Private Debian-based operating system you can run on your existing Apple/Windows PC that boots up off a flash drive or DVD allowing you to bypass the existing OS.

Censorship-Resistent and (ideally) Distributed File Storage

InterPlanetary File System (IPFS) – Censorship-resistant distributed file system,

SyncThing - Open source, decentralized data synchronization

Data Security - Applications That Frustrate Organized Crime "Government's" ~~Taxation~~ Theft and Spying

Vericrypt - free open source disk encryption software for Windows, Mac OSX and Linux, based on TrueCrypt 7.1a.

Ripley, Prey, and uLocker – Tools that instantly secure and encrypt corporate servers, laptops and tablets when government agents enter a business.

Open Source (some decentralized) Social Media and Video Sharing Platforms - The goal is to have a trusted open source social media and video hosting platforms that ideally pays/revenue shares with creators in crypto with good governance, treasury and is decentralized so that it can't be taken down by any organized crime governments. If the platform is enforcing DMCA and can censor content ad-hoc then we don't consider it "decentralized", but we would accept community standards (no child pornography, snuff films, etc.) enforced by random assignment to a community jury in a transparent process.
Mastadon (Our Page)- Decentralized, open-source micro-blogging engine that you can run on your own server.
Pocketnet.app (Our Page)- Open source and decentralized social media platform with crypto payments
ISEGoria – Ben Swann's upstart media platform that pays creators in crypto currencies (start-up, fund-raising)
Flote.app (Our Page)- Open source (but not decentralized) social media platform
Minds.com (Our Page) - Open source social media, but not decentralized
Mewe.com (Our Page)- Open source social media
SteemIt.com (Our Page)– Censorship resistant blockchain reddit that monetizes content for creators in cryptocurrency.
LBRY (Our Page)– Open source, decentralized content platform. Doesn't take down but enforces DMCA by flagging takedown requests which their apps then delist.
Completely Untrusted: Twitter (Our Page), Facebook (Our Page), Reddit, - Caught censoring
Too Suspicious to List: GAB (Our Page) and Dissenter -Failed our testing, suspicious founder, too much mainstream press,

Cryptocurrency Exchanges - Non-Know Your Customer (KYC) Crypto Exchanges - "Know Your Customer" is a law passed by the organized crime US government requiring US-based crypto exchanges, banks and brokerages to capture driver's license and other identifying information so everyone can be tracked, traced, and taxed. Here is a list of crypto exchanges that don't require KYC: https://fuk.io/no-kyc-exchanges-list/
Sideshift.ai and Changelly.com- On-the-fly crypto exchanges that are alternatives to ShapeShift, which now requires KYC.
Local Bitcoin Cash - A way of buying and selling Bitcoin Cash anonymously where participants can meet in person (or transact over the internet) and buy/sell without KYC requirements now that LocalBitcoins.com requires KYC and did away with in-person trades.

Cryptocurrency Mixers and Tumblers - A cryptocurrency tumbler or cryptocurrency mixing is a service offered to mix potentially identifiable cryptocurrency funds with others, with the intention of confusing the trail back to the fund's original source. Tumblers have arisen to improve the anonymity of cryptocurrencies and typically charge a small fee for the service.
XMR.to - A service that allows you to spend anonymous monero with merchants that only accept Bitcoin by allowing you to send Monero and specify the address of the payee who will be sent BTC.
BCH CashShuffle and upcoming **Cashfusion** - CashShuffle anonymizes your coins by mixing them. CashFusion allows you to put those coins back together without ruining the privacy. With CashShuffle, your coins are split up into smaller amounts. You can't put those coins back together or spend them together without ruining the privacy. Cash Fusion fixes that by letting you put your coins back together and keep your privacy.

Anonymous Digital Cash Projects

Unlike Bitcoin whose transactions are visible on a public blockchain, anonymous digital cash refers to crypto-currency projects that use a variety of technologies to obfuscate the origins, amounts and destinations of all transactions while maintaining the decentralized nature that prevents take-downs and the verifiability of transactions that prevents double-spending, counterfeiting and inflation.

Anonymous Cash Projects	Overview	Info, Audit and/or 3rd Party Review
Monero getmonero.org	Monero uses multiple technologies to obfuscate the origins, amounts, and destinations of all transactions. Decentralized	https://blog.quarkslab.com/security-audit-of-monero-randomx.html
Dash - Private Sends dash.org	Dash is a decentralized crypto-currency with a feature called: PrivateSend that "mixes" Dash coins so external observers can't see source of coins.	https://docs.dash.org/en/stable/wallets/dashcore/privatesend-instantsend.html
Grin (GRIN) https://grin.mw/	Grin is a MimbleWimble-based cryptocurrency that aims to offer all users the ability to use electronic transactions without censorship or restrictions. The main idea is to empower anyone to transact or save modern money without the fear of external control or oppression.	https://coinspect.com/grin-security-audit/
ZCash https://z.cash/	Like Bitcoin, Zcash transaction data is posted to a public blockchain; but unlike Bitcoin, Zcash ensures that personal and transaction data remain confidential. Zero-knowledge proofs allow transactions to be verified without revealing the sender, receiver or transaction amount. Selective disclosure features within Zcash allow a user to share some transaction details, for purposes of compliance or audits	https://electriccoin.co/blog/audit-results/

Cryptocurrency - Software Wallets and Crypto Payment Solutions Focused on Digital Liberty

BTCPay Server - Self-hosted, open-source cryptocurrency payment processor with no fees or third-parties featuring point-of-sale and website integration with WooCommerce, Drupal, Presta and others.

Samourai - Software bitcoin wallet focused on privacy that can mask payment details from blockchain explorers and can synch with your own (optional) Dojo full node server, a hardware device that simplifies running a full BTC node meaning that you aren't broadcasting transactions over the net. Your connecting to your own personal node.

Wasabi Wallet - Open-source, non-custodial, privacy-focused Bitcoin wallet for Desktop, that implements trustless coin shuffling with mathematically provable anonymity.

Cryptocurrency - Secure Open Source Hardware Wallets, Secure Mining & Nodes

IOU.Guru - Open source cryptocurrency hardware wallet that instantly prints easily sweepable paper wallets that can trade in commerce like physical cash.

Nodl Dojo - The nodl Samourai edition is the result of a partnership between Samourai Wallet and nodl to use the Samourai Wallet privately. After you pair your Samourai Wallet with the embedded Dojo server through tor, your wallet will use your own Dojo server to process transactions.

Coldcard Hardware Wallets - Secure elements, open source, true air-gap operation, Duress PIN, Brick Me PIN, forced delay, distraction wallets, enables completely offline transactions using partially signed bitcoin txs

OpenDime - USB "Credit Stick"/Bearer Bond for Bitcoin

Mule Tools - alternative ways of broadcasting Bitcoin transactions including sms, fax, telex, hf nodes, meshnets, pdf, satellites, and others.

Free Markets, Darknet, Deepweb and Onion Markets

OpenBazaar - free, semi-decentralized and open source free marketplace.

Haven - Private Shopping mobile app on Android and Apple iOS is the mobile interface with OpenBazaar's decentralized market.

Bitify.com - Like eBay with crypto currency and no KYC (but can't be verified seller)

WeShopwithCrypto.com - New but capable entrant that accepts dozens of coins.

HomesteadersCoop.com - Steemit.com marketplace: pay with STEEM, SBD, BTC, and ETH direct to seller's wallet.

SwarmCity – Decentralized marketplace for services paid with crypto. (Working Beta)

Forra.io - front-end for Ebay vs. a marketplace of its own. You can list and sell items only there. no search function for things listed directly on Forra, it only has a search for items on Ebay. Also, sellers don't have a store for their products.

Darknet/Deepweb/Onion Markets - Darknet markets are accessed through the TOR Browser which bounces requests through multiple serves to obscure IP addresses. It is believed that the intelligence agencies are monitoring exit nodes. Please suggest TOR alternatives through our ProtonMail account or Trello board.
https://www.deepwebsiteslinks.com/deep-web-markets-links/

Important: These recommendations for trusted and secure alternatives are a compilation of suggestions from the author and members of the Art of Liberty Foundation community. The author(s) are unable to vouch 100% for the security of even open source projects because we, currently, lack the resources to investigate / verify the code bases, but could if funding developed (Serious Inquires Only). We are crowd-sourced and we have set up a Trello board to track each of these recommendations and allow trusted, vetted members of the community to make suggestions and/or provide feedback.
https://trello.com/b/bNvqHIDT/freedom-apps-blockchain-and-crypto-solutions

Grid-Down, Internet-Down, Economic Collapse, Open Tyranny and Personal Security Situations

US Dollar Alternatives - Timebanking is a time-based currency. Give one hour of service to another, and receive one time credit. You can use the credits in turn to receive services — or you can donate them to others.

Community Currencies - Community currencies are money accepted on a local basis, frequently earned by community service, and spendable with participating businesses.

Coinflation.com - Calculators to understand the melt value of current US coins and pre-1965 silver coins (junk Silver) that could be used as money in a currency crisis.

Mesh Networking - Mesh networks are IP networks that use commodity wi-fi routers whose range can be enhanced by homemade directional antennas / even "cantennas" made from Pringles cans to create networks if the organized crime government turns off or censors the internet. Hong Kong protesters are using the Bridgefy app to create mesh networks using their cell phone's bluetooth connections.

Bridgefy - Mesh networking for mobile apps that connects devices via bluetooth to circumvent attempts to shut down internet connectivity.

GoTenna - Wireless mesh networking devices that wirelessly connect to your smartphone and then to other GoTenna wireless devices to create a longer range mesh network than bluetooth. **Suspicious:** Funded by Bilderberg Peter Thiel's Founder Fund

2nd Amendment & Self-Defense Solutions

Ghost Gunner 3 – Personal 3D Milling Machine for AR-9/15/45/308 Lowers, 1911 Pistols, Polymer 80 offering compatibility with Glock® 19/23 Gen3 components and new for 2020: AK-47s

Cell 411 - Crowdsource your emergency! Phone app and optional panic buttons that broadcast your emergency to your custom list of friends, family, neighbors, and/or Five Group/Freedom Cell.

Finding Others

Freedom Cell Connector - Freedom Cells are peer to peer groups organizing themselves in a decentralized manner with the collective goal of asserting the sovereignty of group members through peaceful resistance and the creation of alternative institutions.

PrepperGroups.com & **PrepperLink.com** - Websites that help new survivalists find survivable retreats or partnerships with others. OPSEC is advised!

If you would like to be a contributor to this Trello board, provide feedback on our suggestions, offer alternatives, or donate to test and validate solutions then please contact us at UoSlavery@ProtonMail.com

You + Five Friends

Five is our movement and advice to create a peaceful and voluntary society. Shift 5% of your time from entertainment to education, educate 5 friends, get together at least 5 times a year to help others, and contribute 5% (time or treasure) to worthy causes. And then we win.

Shift 5% – We are awash in sedentary entertainment. Shift 5% of sedentary entertainment/infotainment into active learning, nonfiction reading, or just documentaries instead of sitcoms. Binge books. Study an Issue.

Multiply x 5 - Educate 5 more people... and then have them educate five more. Create a "freedom cell" of 5 friends for edification, fellowship, movie nights and parties.

Get Together x 5 - Commit to helping others, meeting others, or learning from others at least 5Xs a year. It can be a conference or a soup kitchen, a protest or a town hall.

Study 5% - Try to carve out just 5% of your time each week for studying a topic of your interest. "The truth is not for all men, but only for those who seek it." - Ayn Rand

Donate 5% – Voluntaryism is about helping others and taking responsibility for our own communities.

Give Small: Through micro-donations and donation aggregators like Patreon and Bitbacker.io it is possible to easily support a dozen worthy individuals or organizations for $12 a month. Consistent income is the lifeblood of the arts, independent media producers, and the developing alternative media. No gift is too small if it is regular and dependable.

Give Time: Find a meet up, charity, nonprofit, or civic organization where you are involved at the grass roots level

Give Big: If you can afford it then consider supporting freedom and the liberty movement in a big way. Water a thousand flowers as long as they are authentic.

Thoughts on strategy:

1. We win the free market meritocracy and "Influential Sneezers" and they positively influence the rest of society. We don't have to win everyone. Just the 10-15% of society in the position to positively influence others: Entrepreneurs, writers, professors, media, content creators, bloggers, vloggers, and activists

2. Water the authentic voices of the growing alternative media Corbett Report, Tragedy & Hope, The Highwire, *your favorites*, etc.

3. Patron the foundations and programs focused on free market economics, liberty, clean food, free market health, scientific truth and personal freedom: Advocates for Self-Government, Mises Institute, Foundation for Economic Education, Fluoride Action Network, The Conscious Resistance Network, We Do Better!, Architects and Engineers for 9-11 Truth, Vaxxed! From a free market charity perspective, we especially like *We Do Better!* which is organizing charitable voucher campaigns that redirect stolen tax dollars away from inefficient State government programs into individual charities. This program has been proven in Arizona where in 2016 130,000 tax filers were able to redirect more than $52 million to 811 state-approved charities which are typically 2-3xs as efficient as the organized crime government.

4. Focus on Efforts Exposing Inter-Generational Organized Crime's Role in Government & Media: The *Art* of Liberty Foundation, 5 (Five), and *"Government"-The Biggest Scam in History Exposed*.

5. Focus some effort on freeing New Hampshire: Free State Project and The Pre-State Project - Our plan to create 25,000 new voluntaryists in New Hampshire by widely exposing organized crime's control of government and media with book and flash drive drops

THE *ART* OF LIBERTY FOUNDATION

The *Art* of Liberty Foundation is a start-up public policy organization focused on:

- Spreading voluntaryist/libertarian ideas through effective media tailored to visual learners, busy people, and short attention spans.
- Exposing inter-generational organized crime's control of the government and media and their use of "government" and Statism as techniques to rob and control the population

Economics

Start Up Mode - $100K Seed ($70K closed)

- Funds R&D & Fundraising A Round

$500K A Round + $150K Pre-State Test

- $500K Start-up voluntaryist public policy organization in New Hampshire
  - Yr1 Anchor staff and facilities
- $150K Pre-State Project – Single Community Test
  - Mail 8,000 to FSP + 3500 HS Seniors/Parents
  - + 500 NH Influential
  - 2 Town Hall Meetings + Documentary Screening

The Foundation produces, curates and distributes books, blogs, podcasts, memes, videos, infographics, and monographs that explain the basics of voluntaryist/libertarian ideas and expose the illogic, illegitimacy and immorality of "government" in addition to its criminality and corruption. The Foundation is focused on developing viral and uncensorable methods of spreading voluntaryist/libertarian news and content and evidence of government and media criminality through hand-to-hand distribution of innovative physical objects including low-cost "picture books", Data DVDs and USB flash drives. The Foundation is currently raising a $50,000 seed round to accelerate these efforts.

Strategy

- Tailor media to "visual learners" and accelerate their time-to-Insight
- Get around internet censorship with uncensorable distribution of physical books, flash drives, and DVDs that also improve readability and comprehension with permanence, visualizations, and infographics that reveal historical patterns of the shady people, banks, cartel companies and organizations that are benefiting from government redistribution & spending, never-ending war and usuries interest on public debt.
- Principled voluntaryist defense of "government" illegitimacy, individual rights, free markets, and voluntary solutions
- **Media, Search & Social Media Watchdog:** Tracking ownership, consolidation, and "government"/"intelligence agency" involvement in coordinated programs across dozens or hundreds of ostensibly independent media properties.
- We promote town hall events, meet ups, conferences, parties, and other real world events that introduce voluntaryists and libertarians to their communities in a positive light

The Pre-State Project

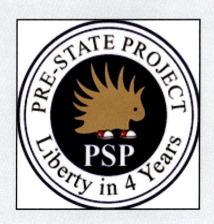

The Pre-State project is our effort to free a single US State from "government" by widely exposing:

- The illegitimacy, illogic, and immorality of "government"
- The apparent involvement of inter-generational organized crime in the creation of the US federal "government" and its on-going and now obviously criminal operations
- The use of unethically manipulative "educational" methods like Statism, government affiliated youth programs and obedience techniques in the mandatory government schools in addition to the debilitation of the government's mandatory mercury and aluminum-laced vaccines.
- Organized crime's control-of-perception program using a handful of monopoly media companies operating as a cartel and major internet search and social media companies on the DARPA internet
- The voluntaryist libertarian alternative of free markets, voluntary associations, tolerance, peaceful civil disobedience and secession.

Background: The **Free** State Project is an effort by voluntaryist and libertarian-leaning freedom activists to move to a single State, New Hampshire, with a history of liberty and a population low-enough where a migration or concentration of freedom-activists could affect real change. The **Pre**-State Project is our effort to accelerate the objectives of the Free State Project by widely exposing organized crime's control system and offering the voluntaryist alternative of real freedom, non-violence, tolerance, and peace. The goal is to introduce 25,000 of the libertarian-leaning among existing New Hampshire residents to voluntaryism, real freedom and activism through effective distribution of physical books, Liberator flash drives, and DVD documentaries in a campaign that would promote town hall meetings where we would introduce the liberty-oriented social and political networks in the state.

> Economics
>
> Cost to Test in a Single Community in New Hampshire (NH): **$150,000**
>
> - 2 Packages to 4,000 Free State Project Members – 1 for them, 1 for friend
> - 1 Package to 3,500 high-school seniors + parents + 3 "Town Hall" events in a single school district
> - 1 package to 500 NH Influential + press
>
> Cost to Mail/Deliver 100,000 copies in 12 NH communities + 3 Town Hall Meetings in Each Community: **$1,000,000**

Why is New Hampshire "the Achilles Heel" of Statism? In addition to having a history of individual liberty and a relatively small proportion of people that work for either the state or federal government, New Hampshire has the densest concentration of libertarians in the country. The Free State Project has been on the ground since 2003, its members host 550 Meet-Ups a year in every corner of the state, and has almost 5,000 activists on the ground with an additional 20,000+ that have pledged to move including 1300+ that pledged last year. 343 moved in 2018 and more arrive every week. In addition to the Free State Project there are a myriad of liberty-oriented organizations working on everything from secession to police accountability to putting liberty-oriented mini-libraries in laundromats. In short, New Hampshire has the social and political networks to absorb, educate, and organize new libertarians in provenly effective ways. It's the perfect place to achieve the "100th Monkey Effect" where a majority of the population adopts new knowledge somewhat simultaneously. Goal: Peaceful and orderly secession from the US and/or widespread Gandhi / Martin Luther King-esque civil disobedience that can't be ignored by the rest of the country. We can win freedom everywhere but first we have to win somewhere and we believe that somewhere is New Hampshire! We believe that, once successful, New Hampshire can serve as a template, laboratory and "proof-of-concept" for prosperous and harmonious voluntaryist societies.

Read our detailed Executive Summary Here: https://www.scribd.com/document/386192564/Art-of-Liberty-Foundation-Pre-State-Project-Executive-Summary-December-2018?secret_password=CNxjzPdOKO1ASJgy8LIp

The Liberator – Our Flash Drive of Liberty Resources

The Liberator – A viral flash drive/Dropbox/Data DVD full of liberty resources that both expose the control system and provide the healthy alternatives of voluntaryism/anarchy, freedom, love, tolerance, agorism, counter-economics, and crypto-currencies. The Liberator includes the PDF version of *"Government" - The Biggest Scam in History Exposed* and the interactive overview poster that looks great on the interactive smart boards in the government's mandatory indoctrination centers. Download from our Dropbox to create your own flash drives or Data DVDs.

A SAMPLING OF THE CONTENTS:
Important Books: *The Most Dangerous Superstition* by Larken Rose, *War is a Racket* by Maj General Smedley Butler USMC, *For a New Liberty – The Libertarian Manifesto* by Murray Rothbard, *Wall Street and the Bolshevik Revolution* – Antony Sutton
Important Short Videos: Statism: The Most Dangerous Religion, The Conversation, The Philosophy of Liberty, 5 Questions – Government on Trial, The Myth of Authority (Video Contest Winner), A Jaw-Dropping History Lesson on the US Dollar – Absolutely Forbidden in Schools by Brian Young, The Biggest Secret of the Secret Service - They Know "Government" is Organized Crime - Etienne de la Boetie2
Articles: How the CIA made Google by Nafeez Ahmed, and, Mapping the Swamp (Exorbitant Salaries of Federal "workers"), Sterilization Chemicals Found in Vaccines, Research Proves Google Manipulated Millions to Promote Clinton
Government School, Police/Military Indoctrination and Brainwashing: 5 Ways Public Schools Brainwash Children, The Engineered School System – John Taylor Gatto Interview, The Military is a Cult! and How and Why Military Basic Training Brainwashes Recruits
The Hidden Propaganda of The Monopoly Media: CNN Fake Charles Jaco Gulf War One Newscast, Fake Baghdad Statue Toppling(2003), Oklahoma City Bombing Vanishing News of Multiple Bombs, Canadian Police Caught Inciting Violence Pretending to Be "Anarchists"
Documentaries: Century of Enslavement by James Corbett, Waco – A New Revelation, America-From Freedom to Fascism, Vaxxed – Trailer on Liberator, Official Viewing on Website, 9-11 Explosive Evidence – Experts Speak Out – One Hour Free Version
Dank Liberty Memes: Too many to list! Check Em Out on DropBox
Visualizations: The Network of Global Corporate Control (2011), Monopoly Media Ownership Chart, Foundations Fund Leftist Media, 2017 Swiss Propaganda Research Bilderberg, CFR, and Trilateralist in Media Chart, 2010 FREE Bilderberger, CFR and Trilateralist in Everything Chart
Truth Music from the movement's leading artists including: Alais Clay, BurntMD, DISL Automatic, Eric July and Backwardz, The Founders, The Freenauts, Jordan Page, Remo Conscious, Rob Hustle, Tatiana Moroz, Truniversal, and Wandering Monks.
Make Your Own Liberators: Anyone can download the contents of the Liberator right from our DropBox to a flash drive with at least 8GB of memory or a DVD-R DL 8.5 GB blank disc. You can download the printable labels to wrap both flash drives and DVDs from the Liberator formatted for widely available Avery labels. Contribute flash drives through our Flash Drives for Freedom-USA Chapter effort that we will wipe, load up with Liberty content and distribute.

"Resistance is the difference between being enslaved and being a slave." – EdlB2

The Symbolism Behind the Liberator

The 1942 Liberator pistol was a $2.10 single-shot pistol that the US dropped to the resistance in occupied France in World War II similar to our distribution of Liberty material on inexpensive flash drives in the occupied USA. The gun came in a cardboard box with ten .45 caliber ACP rounds, a wooden dowel to extract spent shell casings, and an infographic showing how to load and shoot the gun.

Our version features a white Lotus growing from the barrel in a universal symbol of peace to make it clear that we respect the "Golden Rule" and [Non-Aggression Principal](#) (NAP), aren't advocating any violence, and simply recycling organized crime's own iconography against them.

Symbolically, the Lotus represents the ability for everyone to better themselves no matter their current circumstances through constant self-improvement the way the Lotus flower grows beautifully from the muck. It is our peace offering to everyone who serves/has served: "The System." Even if you were tricked by *mandatory* indoctrination and *paid-for propaganda* to murder foreign or domestic, SWAT-team and cage overwhelmingly peaceful people for victimless crimes, indoctrinate children or propagandize the population from Hollywood, New York, Washington DC, Atlanta or Langley..

It's OK... everyone can be forgiven, everyone can leave the cult of Statism and its poisonous ideas behind, and be born again into a beautiful, non-violent, free-thinking human being.

The final symbolism of the *Liberator* is that because, in many cases, we are dealing with mind-controlled, non-critical-thinking "order-followers" who were *unethically and manipulatively* trained by an organized crime system to falsely believe they have rights that mere mortals do not and just can't seem to understand that not everyone believes in their *artificially indoctrinated Statist religion*... then the smartest thing to do is to: *Hold on to the Gun!*

Large Scale Cult Deprogramming & Uncensorable Hand-to-Hand Distribution
What, Why, and How to Help!

> Cult - \ 'kəlt \ noun, often attributive - *A cult is a group or movement exhibiting a great or **excessive devotion** or dedication to some person, idea, or thing and **employing unethically manipulative techniques of persuasion and control** (e.g., isolation from former friends and family, debilitation, use of special methods to heighten suggestibility and subservience, powerful group pressures, information management, suspension of individuality or critical judgment, promotion of total dependency on the group and fear of leaving it, etc.) **designed to advance the goals of the group's leaders to the actual or possible detriment of members, their families, or the community**.*

Confucius famously said that *"The beginning of wisdom is to call things by their proper name."* Using the word "cult" unfortunately seems to offend some but the stone-cold truth is that is exactly the dynamic at play. If the problem is inter-generational organized crime using control of government schools, scouting, military/police training, and a weaponized media propaganda system to perpetrate *classic, textbook unethically manipulative* "cult indoctrination techniques" on an unsuspecting population then the solution must be: **Large Scale Cult Deprogramming** starting with calling the problem by its rightful name.

1st Image: Shave-headed police recruits dressed in identical costumes being taught that they have rights that others don't and that its ok for them to use violence on peaceful people and arrest/cage people for victimless crimes. **2nd Image:** From the LA Times: March 29, 1943: Vierling Kersey, superintendent of schools, left, and Roy J. Becker, Board of Education president, demonstrate old and new methods of saluting Old Glory. The new hand-over-heart method goes in effect in schools on Army Day. **Monkey See, Monkey Do!** - **Most people emulate what they see on the weaponized tell-lie-vision. 3rd Image:** Original LA Times Caption: April 12, 1942: Actress Irene Rich leads 4,000 citizens in salute to the flag during program at the Hollywood Bowl. The 4,000 – including several Hollywood celebrities – were sworn in as air-raid wardens, fire watchers, messengers and auxiliary policemen. The flag salute, as shown in this image, was replaced by the hand-over-heart method. [Editor: Government + the media working together to sell statism/patriotism (mental slavery) government bonds, tax slavery, and a foreign war that FDR purposefully provoked.]

Complete Breakdown with Examples

Cult - \ 'kəlt \ noun, often attributive -

A cult is a group or movement exhibiting: a great or excessive devotion or dedication to some person, idea, or thing
- Nylon cloth (the flag), the holy documents of the Constitution, BoR, the concept of government, "The Law" (I.E. politician scribbles)

and employing unethically manipulative techniques of persuasion and control (e.g.,isolation from former friends and family
- Mandatory government schools take kids from family, military bases, commissaries, etc. segment the shave headed enforcers from the rest of society

debilitation
- Hidden curriculum of Statism in schools, scouting, and police/military training, purposefully crappy education with almost zero (0) focus on logic, morality, the real history of the US, and/or the Trivium (Grammar, Logic, and Rhetoric), IQ lowering Fluoride in water, mercury/aluminum in vaccines

use of special methods to heighten suggestibility and subservience
- **Government Schools:** Mandatory gov't "education", can't raise your hand or go to the bathroom without the gov't permission, socialization of enforcement class through D.A.R.E., jROTC, military recruiters in schools, etc.
- **Police/Military:** Obedience to hierarchical authority even over the individuals own consciousness and basic morality, boot camps, police academies, and "basic training"

powerful group pressures
- Enforced social conformity from early age I.E. Forced to stand with hand over heart for pledge and national anthem, forced to fight/murder in foreign occupations to protect friends, police "blue wall of silence"/ police perjury/"testilying"

information management
- Hidden propaganda (Product placement of the flag, anchoring, etc.) in 1000+ television program and 800+ movies, National Public Radio, Voice of America, Armed Forces Radio, the "Echo Chamber" of Fusion Center/ InfraGuard "top secret" intelligence that no one else can verify
- Mandatory gov't schools/tax-supported state universities, police/military "training", secrecy oaths, national security letters,
- Search engine manipulation, state-sponsored "sock-puppet" social media manipulation, "paid for patriotism", and poisoning-the-well of truth news and journalism.

suspension of individuality
- **Gov't Schools:** Everyone's an "American.. It's been decided for you!
- **Police / Military:** Shaved heads similar to other cults, identical costumes (I.E. uni-forms (the single form), badges and patches that signify allegiance to the group, and differentiation from others), willingness to commit violence with/for the group

or critical judgment
- Statist obedience to "The Law" (politician scribbles) over their own judgement or basic morality, obedience to hierarchical authority, "order following" "I don't make the Jim Crow/Fugitive slave/plant possession laws.. I just enforce them!", "tax payer" willingness to pay any level of taxation however damaging to family's finances.

promotion of total dependency on the group and fear of leaving it, etc.)
- Government employees/police/teachers/military feel trapped by exorbitant salaries and pensions most couldn't get in the private sector (even though everyone would be better off if we rid ourselves of the parasite of organized crime government)

designed to advance the goals of the group's leaders
- Trillions of dollars given to private banks and media companies through the "bailouts" and TARP/TALF program recycled into political contributions to the Congressmen who passed it even though 90%+ of the country opposed it, Trillions missing from Pentagon, Billions from the post office, Amtrak, HUD and other programs. Monopoly privileges, monopoly patent protections, fractional reserve banking's hidden "inflation tax"

to the actual or possible detriment of members(karma), their families(karma), or the community.
- Population "chumped" and "duped" into believing they "owe" taxes (tithes) to organized crime, military's willingness to kill foreigners in foreign wars based on obvious lies, police willingness to cage "non-believers" in for-profit prisons and extort money from their neighbors for victimless crimes and road piracy.

The Art of Liberty Foundation Strategy:
We are going after the visual learners and accelerating their "Time-to-Insight"! - 65% are visual learners who learn best and fastest when they see information. Humans are the world's best pattern recognition machines, and revelation of the control techniques reveals that this system is formulaic, deceitful, and indoctrinated.

We are taking it to the schools - The interactive posters/infographics we are designing are formatted for the hundreds of thousands of interactive touch-screen SMART Boards and Promethean boards in K-12 classrooms and universities. We are producing the interactive program on inexpensive flash drives & wi-fi servers that include other liberty curricula. We call these drives: **The Liberator**.

You can download the contents of the Liberator, including the stickers needed to wrap a blank USB.

- **Innovations:** First effort ever designed to utilize the interactive whiteboards in government classrooms, force multiplier in that one awake kid (or one honest teacher or professor) can take an entire classroom full of students through a high-level overview of the problem with visuals that accelerate understanding and interactivity.

We are accurate and well-referenced - we are aggressively fact-checking and referencing everything with authoritative, scholarly research delivered in a variety of formats (website, documentaries) for individual learning preferences. We are crowd-sourced, so if you see something incorrect or would like to contribute, please e-mail me at: UoSlavery@ProtonMail.com

We are combating internet censorship by developing viral, uncensorable distribution for truth material - If we know that society is communicating on a DARPA-funded military network called "The Internet" where organized crime /government affiliated search engines, social media platforms, and monopoly media companies are controlling the flow of information with "filter bubbles", "sock puppets", search result manipulation, demonetization of independent media content, and other ways, many imperceptible to the masses, then the solution must entail uncensorable, viral, hand-to-hand distribution of truth content and wi-fi "Freedom Box" file servers.

- **Innovations:** Every Liberator has instructions and printable stickers to create new flash drive or DVD Liberators. Stickers can be printed on readily available full sheet label paper.

We are looking to be well-funded - We are looking to partner with "idea-philanthropists" and liberty donors interested in getting hundreds of thousands (millions?) of students exposed to the ideas of liberty, and we are exploring crowd-funding this effort to ensure we are well-capitalized for accuracy, impact, and viral growth.

We are making it fun to organize! The *Art* of Liberty Foundation promotes making it fun to organize with unique events that bring people together and supercharge them.

The Art of Liberty on the Beach – An annual fund raiser for the Foundation that drew almost 400 attendees to our favorite turtle sanctuary outside of Acapulco in 2019. Our friends enjoyed a magical evening on the beach with a bonfire, coconut drinks, fireworks, and some of the truth movement's leading artists including Alais Clay, Freenauts Ela Mental, and DJ Koala.

Get the *"Government" - The Biggest Scam in History Exposed* Poster for your High School or College Classroom

With the book *"Government" - The Biggest Scam in History Exposed*, we tried to keep it short and use images to accelerate and deepen understanding.
With the poster we are doing the same thing condensed to a single large format overview that can be displayed on interactive Smartboards in high school and college classrooms. Larken Rose's 5 Questions are also prominently on the poster!

The downloadable, printable PDF can be found on our viral Dropbox and/or USB thumbdrive: **The Liberator**
Get the poster, PDF of the book, and the rest of the Liberator contents here:
www.Government-Scam.com/liberator

International Editions - On the Horizon !

Think of the various countries of the world as different tax farms where inter-generational organized crime has been farming human labor and controlling society using variations of the same mafia mandatory government schools, cub scouts, boy scouts, jROTC, police/military model. They are all using essentially the same techniques including monopoly government money, statism, propaganda and spying on everyone in each country and the same program that produced jack-booted Nazi cult-members / "order followers" marching in formation in 1930s Germany produces jack-booted cult-member "order followers" marching in formation today in the US, UK, Russia, Israel, China, and North Korea.

We would like to publish international editions where we swap out the East German examples in this edition with the specifics of each modern country. We are looking to partner with liberty donors and "Idea Philanthropists" interested in funding local, translated editions specific to each country with a "Flash Drives for Freedom" program with evidence of that country's criminality. Please consider passing this along to the liberty donors and liberty-oriented think tanks and public policy organizations in our targeted countries.

Soft Cover Edition
$30 USA Domestic - Postage Paid USPS Media Mail
$35 USA Domestic - Postage Paid USPS Flat Rate Envelope
$75 International – USPS International Priority Mail

The Liberator Flash Drive - Preloaded
$17.76 Single Liberator – Postage Paid USPS First Class Mail
$25.00 for Two Liberators – USA Domestic – Postage Paid USPS First Class Mail
$70 International – USPS International Priority Mail

Book + Flash Drive Combo
$43 USA Media Mail
$50 USA USPS Priority Mail
$79 International Orders Delivered using USPS Intl Envelope.

THE LIBERATOR – LARGE
INCLUDES . . .

COMING SOON

Perfect for **Educating**:
- A Single Government Classroom
- A Scout Troop
- A Platoon of Soldiers
- A Neighborhood
- A Business or Farm

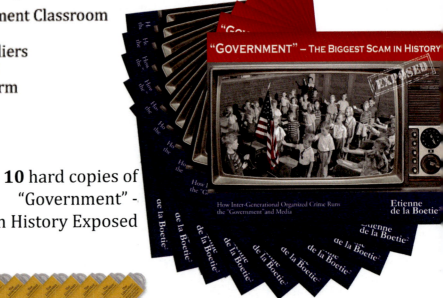

10 hard copies of "Government" - The Biggest Scam in History Exposed

35 Liberator USB Thumbdrives

[Order the Book- Soft Cover]   [Order the Liberator]   [Order the Combo]

THE LIBERATOR – EXTRA LARGE
INCLUDES...

Perfect for Educating:
- An Entire School
- An Entire Military Base
- A Boy Scout Jamboree
- A JROTC or ROTC Unit
- A US Military Academy

NOTE: We are looking for Idea Philanthropists interested in getting the cost down and effectiveness up!

20 hard copies of "Government" – The Biggest Scam in History Exposed

Mini-Library of Books & DVDs for your:
- School Library
- Military Base Library
- Military Academy Library
- Community Library
- Private "Pop-Up" Community Library/Liberty Tree
- Company Lunch Room
- Boy Scout Troop Library

100 Liberator USB Thumbdrives

Mini Library Includes:

Documentaries
- Vaxxed DVD
- The Greater Good DVD
- Anatomy of a Great Deception DVD
- Explosive Evidence: Experts Speak Out DVD
- Century of Enslavement DVD
- Sir! No Sir! DVD

Books
- An Underground History of American Education by John Taylor Gatto
- Anatomy of the State by Murray Rothbard
- The Most Dangerous Superstition by Larken Rose
- War is a Racket by Smedley Butler
- The Creature from Jekyll Island by G. Edward Griffin

Sponsorship/Donation/Order Form

I (we) hereby authorize The *Art* of Liberty Foundation, herein after called ORGANIZATION, to initiate debit entries to my (our) Checking Account or Savings Account (select one) indicated below at the depository financial institution named below, hereafter called DEPOSITORY, and to debit the same to such account. I (we) acknowledge that the origination of the ACH transactions to my (our) account must comply with the provisions of the U.S. law.

Please send list of desired products and include phone number and e-mail address.

Bank Account Information

_____
Depository Name

_____
Name on Account

_____
Signature

_____
Routing #

_____
Account #

_____
Date   **Donation Amount**

☐ Checking   ☐ Savings

☐ One time donation   ☐ Monthly donation

Credit Card Information

_____
Name on Card

_____
Signature

_____
Card Number

_____
Expiration Date

_____
Security Code   Zip Code

_____
Date   **Donation Amount**

☐ Master Card   ☐ Visa
☐ Discover   ☐ American Express

☐ One time donation   ☐ Monthly donation

Please scan or photograph and e-mail to: UoSlavery@Protonmail.com

How to Help with CryptoCurrency

Donate Bitcoin Cash:

qqtq4udrl62r62zcmdwwlmgm23yan94tkyz3p0tt00

Donate Bitcoin:

14w1oGqWttvnT14TK4vCxBGsLkKwQ7kg6z

Donate Dash:

XoHe5k9Ahmuc8rja41orVWrKcqS3Z9CbYb

Donate Ethereum:

0xdb29c1d10b543d8d34b73a1ef72dc6afd6315b55

Donate Monero:

48LaiPi2AXSfkSPVEG16jrMJ5TzDhxE1HeYvoyLS8w-CxPzuz2tGg6srQENyjs4RaFZZFceWq3rxd7cN8Me5aFtKNQdYXuzL?tx_payment_id=dd99918c6565347d

QR Code opens our Steemit Page:

https://steemit.com/@uoslavery

Dedication

This book is dedicated to all the victims of government indoctrination, their victims, and to the **few,** rapidly developing into the many, with the courage to speak up and fight back!

Acknowledgements

This is the 4th edition and 5th printing of a book that I "rapidly prototyped" as *Understanding Your Slavery* in 2017, then *Understanding Our Slavery,* and now *"Government"*. There is original research but I must confess that I stand on the shoulders of giants. I simply could not have done this work without the help intellectually, spiritually and financially of so many amazing people in the liberty and truth communities. There are some that stand out: Ron Paul for turning me on to libertarianism in 1988, Tom Palmer for allowing me to audit his classes at Cato which ignited my love of liberty and the free market and to Ayn Rand, Murray Rothbard, Milton and David Friedman, Tom Woods, Walter Block, Frederick Bastiat, Rose Wilder Lane, Ludwig Von Mises, Harry Browne, David Boaz, and Mary Ruwart for deepening it. To Marshall Fritz, John Taylor Gatto, & David James Rodriguez for exposing the hidden curriculum of the education system. To Vernie Kuglin, Irwin Shiff, and Aaron Russo for explaining the fraud and criminality of the IRS and tax system. To Ken W. for taking a chance on me with my first job & giving me a deep understanding of technology. To Jo Jorgensen for giving me an in-depth understanding into how corrupt and rigged the two-party system vs. 3rd parties. To George Gilder and Shawn M. for getting me into internet business, Stafford and Ian B. for sending me to Wall Street and to Mike C. & Richard M. for teaching me how it worked. To the Mindshare CEO network in DC for a glimpse into how DC works. To Herold W. and David M. for putting up with me in business ventures. To Mark Passio for teaching me about Natural Law and the Great Work. To the Advocates for Self-Government, the Foundation for Harmony and Prosperity, the Foundation for Economic Education, The Free State Project, & the Mises Institute for creating so many fellow voluntaryists & libertarians. To Larken Rose (& Amanda)for opening the final door to voluntaryism and anarchy and putting the final piece in the puzzle: Statism IS a religion. To Anam Paiseanta for helping me let go of my anger. To Derrick Broze (and Miriam!) and Kenny Palurintano for raising my consciousness and karma, to Cary Wedler and Clark Kozak for helping edit and fact-check the 2nd edition of the book & work on the websites. To James Corbett, Richard Grove (and Lisa A.!), Ernie Hancock (& Donna!), and Brian Young for researching just about everything and making it easy-to-consume. To Richard Gage, Chris Bollyn, Dan Dicks, Jess Baldock, and David Hooper for exposing 9-11. To Kenneth Royce for exposing the fraud of the Con-stitution & Rex Curry for exposing the shady history of the pledge of allegiance. To Ole Dammegard, Max Igan, Mr. Stosh, Plasmaburns, Sonofnewo, Jim Fetzer, Kevin Barrett, and Independent Media Solidarity for helping me understand false flag terror & hoax shootings. To William Gazecki, Dan Gifford, and Michael McNulty for exposing the govt's massacre at Waco. To RFK Jr., Del Bigtree, Andrew Wakefield, Kendall Nelson, Leslie Manookian, Eric Gladen, & Dr. Mercola for exposing the scientific fraud of the government's mercury & aluminum-laced vaccines. To Dr. Paul Connett & Dr. William Hirzy who explained the scam of Fluoride. To Smedley Butler, the Wise Sloth, Doug Valentine & Fat Leonard for exposing the criminality of the military/CIA. To Catherine Austin Fitts, Dr. Mark Skidmore, and Dr. Paul Craig Roberts, Bill Still, & G. Edward Griffin for explaining inflation and exposing the theft of Trillions. To Roger Ver for giving me a tier-one lesson on crypto over dinner which convinced me to give my boys their allowance in BTC. To Bruce Baumann, Nate Henderson, Truniversal, Alais Clay, Freenauts, DJ Koala, Ela Mental, Monica and Michele at Campamento Tortuguero Playa Hermosa, and everyone else who helps co-create the Turtle Party! To Jordan Page, DISL Automatic, Nahko, Rob Hustle, Neema V, W. Monks and other freedom artists. To Lisa K., Shelby K., and the tireless & multi-talented Miriam Zachariah who helped make this book look so good! To My Friends and Family: Aaron R., Amber R., Audrey H., Bill R., Carolyn W. D., Casey C., Corby W., Dave H., David L., Jane K., Jen A., Joel W., John G., Kent W., Kristi W., Mike L., Ron A., Thomas N., Kara R., Kevin G., Kyle H., Theresa L., and Vickie W., for putting up with me for decades, to Chris R., Robert Murray, Jimmy Calfee., Z. Zameron, Andy H. and all the other donors to the *Art* of Liberty Foundation who have helped fund this peaceful revolution of ideas. Finally, to my sons: Rand, Jaxon, & Carter who inspire me to push on to ensure their future is one of liberty, prosperity and *real* freedom!

Connect with Us on E-mail and Social Media

We are using the intelligence agencies manipulated social media platforms including Facebook, YouTube, and Twitter for now and are publishing on more trustworthy open-source, transparent platforms like: BitChute(etienneb2) GAB (Etienne_Boetie2) , Flote.app(etienne), LBRY (lbry://@ArtOfLiberty#a) Mastadon(https://mastodon.the-liberator.news/), Mewe.com (etienneboetie2), Minds.com(EdlBoetie2), Pocketnet.app(etiennedelaboetie2), SteemIt.com (@uoslavery)

Because many, many other truth activists have had their accounts deleted, frozen, shadow banned, and demonetized **if you really want to keep up with our efforts and our content then please subscribe via e-mail.**

We have two e-mail options:
Weekly – Five Meme Friday! where we send out five new hard hitting memes and the occasional new "One-Pagers" sample below:
The Occasional Newsletter – Only for important announcements!

The History of the Etienne de la Boetie[2] Nom de Plume

The original Etienne de la Boetie, 1530-1563, was a French political philosopher who wrote The Discourse of Voluntary Servitude (popularly reprinted in English as: The Anti-Dictator) in the 16th century where he argued that men are not so enslaved as they enslave themselves and the only power tyrants have is given to them by the majority of their victims. He was one of the first to chronicle the techniques that monarchs, the organized crime system of that day, used to create obedience and fealty in their tax slaves. He also observed that there were always "a few" who would not bow and "Resolve to serve no more and you are at once freed"

Here are some quotes from the original Discourse of Voluntary Servitude.

It is incredible how as soon as a people become subject, it promptly falls into such complete forgetfulness of its freedom that it can hardly be roused to the point of regaining it, obeying so easily and willingly that one is led to say that this people has not so much lost its liberty as won its enslavement.

It has always happened that tyrants, in order to strengthen their power, have made every effort to train their people not only in obedience and servility toward themselves, but also in adoration.

Resolve to serve no more, and you are at once freed. I do not ask that you place hands upon the tyrant to topple him over, but simply that you support him no longer; then you will behold him, like a great Colossus whose pedestal has been pulled away, fall of his own weight and break into pieces.

Tyrants would distribute largess, a bushel of wheat, a gallon of wine, and a sesterce: and then everybody would shamelessly cry, "Long live the King!" The fools did not realize that they were merely recovering a portion of their own property, and that their ruler could not have given them what they were receiving without having first taken it from them.

Liberty is the natural condition of the people. Servitude, however, is fostered when people are raised in subjection. People are trained to adore rulers. While freedom is forgotten by many there are always some who will never submit.

The dictator does not consider his power firmly established until he has reached the point where there is no man under him who is of any worth. ... This method tyrants use of stultifying their subjects cannot be more clearly observed than in what Cyrus did with the Lydians after he had taken Sardis, their chief city, and had at his mercy the captured Croesus, their fabulously rich king. When news was brought to him that the people of Sardis had rebelled, it would have been easy for him to reduce them by force; but being unwilling either to sack such a fine city or to maintain an army there to police it, he thought of an unusual expedient for reducing it. He established in it brothels, taverns, and public games, and issued the proclamation that the inhabitants were to enjoy them. He found this type of garrison so effective that he never again had to draw the sword against the Lydians. These wretched people enjoyed themselves inventing all kinds of games, so that the Latins have derived the word from them, and what we call pastimes they call ludi, as if they meant to say Lydi. Not all tyrants have manifested so clearly their intention to effeminize their victims; but in fact, what the aforementioned despot publicly proclaimed and put into effect, most of the others have pursued secretly as an end.

Men are like handsome race horses who first bite the bit and later like it, and rearing under the saddle a while soon learn to enjoy displaying their harness and prance proudly beneath their trappings. Men will grow accustomed to the idea that they have always been in subjection, that their fathers lived in the same way; they will think they are obliged to suffer this evil, and will persuade themselves by example and imitation of others, finally investing those who order them around with proprietary rights, based on the idea that it has always been that way.

There are always a **few** better endowed than others, who feel the weight of the yoke and cannot restrain themselves from attempting to shake it off: these are the men who never become tamed under subjection. These are in fact the men who, possessed of clear minds and far-sighted spirit, are not satisfied, like the brutish mass, to see only what is at their feet, but rather look about them, behind and before, and even recall the things of the past in order to judge those of the future, and compare both with their present condition. These are the ones who, having good minds of their own, have further trained them by study and learning. Even if liberty had entirely perished from the earth, such men would invent it. For them slavery has no satisfactions, no matter how well disguised.